Becoming A Who

Hope, Praise,
Holy Communion, and Pr
for Healing

Rev. Harold Goodwin

To Sue, Carlton
AND FAMILY

Harold (& Dot)
Cyndy

Becoming A Whole Person

Hope, Praise,
Holy Communion, and Prayer
for Healing

Rev. Harold Goodwin

Living Word Books

Cordova, Tennessee

Some scripture (indicated NIV) taken from the HOLY BIBLE, NEW INTERNATIONAL VERSION®. Copyright © 1973, 1978, 1984 International Bible Society. Used by permission of Zondervan. All rights reserved. The "NIV" and "New International Version" trademarks are registered in the United States Patent and Trademark Office by International Bible Society. Use of either trademark requires the permission of International Bible Society.

Some scripture (indicated NRSV) taken from the New Revised Standard Version Bible, copyright 1989, Division of Christian Education of the National Council of the Churches of Christ in the United States of America. Used by permission. All rights reserved.

Some scripture taken from *The Message*. Copyright © 1993, 1994, 1995, 1996, 2000, 2001, 2002. Used by permission of NavPress Publishing Group.

Some Scripture quotations (indicated AMP) taken from the Amplified® Bible, Copyright © 1954, 1958, 1962, 1964, 1965, 1987 by The Lockman Foundation. Used by permission." (www.Lockman.org)

Some scripture (indicated KJV) take from the King James Version of the Holy Bible.

ISBN: 978-0-9793079-7-3

Library of Congress Control Number: 2007940729

Living Word Books
Double-Edged Publishing, Inc.
9618 Misty Brook Cove
Cordova, Tennessee 38016

For the word of God is living and active. Sharper than any double-edged sword, it penetrates even to dividing soul and spirit, joints and marrow; it judges the thoughts and attitudes of the heart.
Hebrews 4:12 New International Version (NIV)

www.doubleedgedpublishing.com

Printed in the United States of America

First Printing

This little booklet is dedicated to Dot, my sweetheart, wife, and soul mate. She has brought healing and wholeness into my life for over 60 years.

Harold Goodwin

Contents

Foreword

Sometimes, the spoken word loses its power when it becomes the written word. Not so with these homilies on healing. You will read these words and feel the warmth, the concern, and the compassion that radiates from Harold Goodwin when he speaks to a group, or when you have the privilege of sharing a personal conversation with him.

The focus of these homilies is healing and wholeness...the need and longing of all of us. So here is a treasury of help and guidance. Harold has the unique gift of pastoral care expressed in profound, but clear and simple teaching. Wherever you are on your journey, you will be personally ministered to. Not only so, here is a resource for us to minister to others.

One of the important truths Harold underscores is that relationship...friendship...is a great source of healing and wholeness.

Jerry (my wife) and I have found this to be true in relation to the Goodwins, Harold and Dot. They have been sources of strength and joy as we have shared our walk together. You will feel that, too, as you read these homilies. Harold invites us into his life as he shares his story; he enters ours and because he knows where we are, and he cares enough and is pastorally experienced enough to join us.

I commend this volume. It is a marvelous offer of "one beggar telling another beggar where to find bread."

Maxie D. Dunnam, Chancellor
Asbury Theological Seminary

Acknowledgements

I deeply appreciate working with the Healing Team in the ministry that produced these brief messages on healing: Fred Boone, Mike Blancett, Steve Caldwell, Arelene and Ramon Diaz, Dot Goodwin, Katherine McGory, Katherine and Loyal Murphy III, Nelle Lewis, Paul Lawler, Rebecca Sullivan, and Bob White.

I am grateful for Mickie Dunn's expertise in the typing and retyping of the manuscript for this little book. Also, I am grateful for her typing of every individual homily delivered these past years. She is truly a dedicated Christian and a most competent staff member at Lindenwood.

Becoming A Whole Person

Hope, Praise,
Holy Communion, and Prayer
for Healing

Rev. Harold Goodwin

Introduction

This small volume of homilies or sermons is a compilation of messages delivered on Sunday evenings in the H. Thomas Wood Chapel at Lindenwood Christian Church in Memphis, Tennessee.

The Ministry of Praise, Hope, Holy Communion, and Prayers for Healing was begun in January of 2005 and has continued on the second and fourth Sundays of each month. Every message addresses some aspect of becoming a whole person in Jesus Christ.

During these months we witnessed the healing of numerous people who had come to worship. In a questionnaire completed by some forty people following our first year, it was noted by respondents that some measure of healing had taken place spiritually, emotionally, relationally or physically in their lives. The evaluation forms also produced the following comments:

- "What an authentic and simple approach to helping us become a whole person."
- "This is a special time. It is different from any of the other worship services we have at Lindenwood."
- "You can feel the presence of the Holy Spirit."
- "The messages are always uplifting, positive, and appropriate to my life and my needs."
- "I feel really blessed by being able to share my prayer concerns verbally with Christian friends."
- "I felt a sense of warmth and acceptance!"

In the publishing of these selected messages, it is hoped that many who read them will be blessed with some measure of wholeness and better health: spiritually, emotionally, relationally, or physically.

Rev. W. Harold Goodwin

Becoming A Whole Person
Matthew 4:23, Matthew 9:35, James 5:13-15

Every local church is engaged automatically in the healing ministry even though it may not have a public healing service such as we are beginning here tonight. Jesus promised that he would always be with his followers. See again, the great commission— Matthew 28:18-20. Jesus concludes with His promise, "And remember I am with you always, to the end of the age" (NRSV).

In the same passage, Jesus tells his followers to obey everything he commanded them to do. This included a clear mandate to love one another and to keep on teaching, preaching, and healing. "He sent them out to preach...and to heal the sick" (Luke 9:2, NRSV).

In preaching, teaching, and observing the Sacraments of Baptism and Holy Communion, worship leaders re-present Christ the great physician. In compassion and prayer for one another, Christians are in a real sense re-presenting Christ as the healer. What we are doing here tonight is offering you and others the opportunity to spend some time in praise, prayer, and Holy Communion focusing on the fact that what Jesus wants for each one of us is wholeness of life.

Christ wants for each one of us wholeness of life. Christ wants to heal us in any area of life in which we need to be healed or made whole. Christ wants to bring his healing power, God's grace, into our physical bodies, our emotions, our relationships, as well as our spirits or souls. If something is hurting us, causing distress or disease—Jesus cares about that. He desires to help you. Your church cares, too, and we want to pray with you about your needs.

One of the scriptures read tonight promises us that "the prayer of faith will heal the sick," yet all of us have prayed for a healing that did not occur according to our requests. Was God not listening? Was our faith too weak? Were our prayers not fervent enough? I think not. But I also think it is a fruitless effort to try to find an answer as to why some are healed and others are not. Much of what happens here on our earthly journey will remain a mystery until we are united with our God face to face.

However, I do not believe we can ever say, "Prayer is wasted. My prayers are wasted efforts." Although prayer may not change a situation and give us what we want, prayer—earnest, sincere prayer—always changes us!

Through prayer we become more aware of God's presence. Through prayer we find inner resources and strength we didn't know we possessed. Through prayer we no longer face our fears alone. God is beside us renewing our spirits, restoring our souls. Christ abides within us, helping us carry the burden when it becomes too heavy.

One thing we definitely know is this: God does not deliberately send tragedy and suffering upon us. Although these things happen to us, they are not God's intention for us. Not once in the Gospels does Jesus say that God sends tragedy and pain—either to test us or to punish us. This is an Old Testament concept. Although obstacles or stumbling blocks may occur and prevent full healing on occasion, the New Testament makes it clear—God is always, always on the side of healing, release, and reconciliation.

Scriptures remind us of this. "God sent His Son to save us" (John 3:16, NRSV). Jesus said, "I have come so that you may have life and have it abundantly" (John 10:10 NRSV). In Matthew 9:20-22, we read of a woman who had suffered a hemorrhage or bleeding for twelve years. She gained faith and courage to timidly reach out and touch the hem of Jesus' robe or cloak. Jesus turned and saw her and said, "Take heart, daughter, your faith has made you well" (NRSV).

The Greek word for wellness here is *"sozo"* or *"sozein."* It is interpreted as:

1. "Your faith has made you well" (KJV).
2. "Your faith has healed you" (NIV).
3. "Your faith has restored you to health" (AMP).

Christ is the great physician. He desires wholeness and health for each one of us. Health, wholeness, wellness is more than the absence of disease. Jesus was firmly convinced of His Father's overriding desire for our wholeness and salvation. He denied entirely the idea that sickness was sent by God as a punitive measure. On one occasion, (Matthew 8:2-3, Mark 1:40 and Luke 5:12-13) a leper came to Jesus saying, "Lord, if you choose, you can make me clean" (NRSV). Moved with pity Jesus stretched out

His hand and touched him, saying, "I do choose [certainly I want to heal you] be made clean" (NRSV). Jesus immediately banished any idea that He would not choose to do so.

Wholeness, or becoming a whole person, is just that—a becoming, a process. It involves the totality of our being—spirit, body, mind, emotion, and relationship. God is calling us at every age and every stage of our lives to become a whole person, even in that final stage of life that we call "dying."

Basic to all wholeness is spiritual health. This is the primary issue in healing or wellness. Paul Tournier, Swiss psychiatrist believed that every chronic or acute illness was due, to some degree, to an underlying spiritual unrest or disorder.

Dr. Scott Morris, who spoke at our Journey to Bethany VI in 2003, had this to say: "Sadness and despair, depression and anxiety are filling our doctor's offices every day. These are problems that in the past were brought to the priest or minister, but are now brought to the physician" (*The Commercial Appeal*, 2/3/03).

Forgiveness of sin and release from guilt are crucial in the healing process. Dr. E. Stanley Jones, years ago made a strong statement concerning the connectedness between ones mind, spirit, and body. In his book *Christian Maturity,* he said, "We must give up the notion that God will (bless or make us whole) without our cooperating with him by giving up thoughts and emotions that produce illness. We must denounce the attitude that we can skip the healing of spirit and (receive) the healing of our bodies."

Paul said in Romans 12:1-2, "we are to be transformed by the renewing of our minds" (NRSV). An important part of renewing our minds takes place when we come to the table and partake of Holy Communion. In Luke Chapter 24, Cleophas and the other disciple had their eyes opened and their minds enlightened as to what Jesus' whole ministry was all about. They understood why Jesus died on the cross.

When we gather at the Lord's Table to partake of bread and wine, it is a unique opportunity to bring our insufficiencies to the all-sufficient Christ. Let us think of Holy Communion as a sort of Sacramental Therapy. It is Christ's means of grace communicating health, wholeness, and salvation.

By therapy, I mean that in this experience, the healing process is enhanced and facilitated, spiritually, emotionally, relationally, and physically. It is a sacrament precisely because the risen Christ is present. And by His power and power of the Holy Spirit we become better persons, spiritually, mentally, emotionally, and physically. In my daily and weekly journey of faith, I need the grace of God as experienced in the sacrament of Holy Communion.

Experiencing God's Forgiveness
I John 1:5-9, Psalm 103:1-5, 8-12

Welcome to our second worship service of Praise, Prayer, Holy Communion, and Healing. It is the desire of our Healing Team that we experience the living presence of the "Great Physician" here in our midst, each and every time we meet. If you feel warmth and a joy as a result of being together singing, praying, and sharing Holy Communion, then our time will have been an answer to prayer.

If, after a period of months, participating in this kind of worship, you can begin to answer the following questions in the affirmative it will have been time well spent:

- Am I feeling any better?
- Do I notice any improvement in my mental, physical or spiritual condition?
- Am I being helped in any way to become a "whole person"?
- Am I gaining any insights as to what is going on in my life?

If you can answer "yes" to any of these four questions, then prayers are being answered, and it just might be that the wholeness and healing is taking place in your life as a result of being in God's presence.

Now, you may remember that the last time we worshiped here we quoted Dr. E. Stanley Jones, Methodist minister and missionary, who said that there is a strong connectedness between one's mind, body, and spirit. Jones said, "We must give up the notion that God will bless or make us whole without our cooperating with Him by giving up thoughts and emotions that produce illness. We must denounce the attitude that we can skip the healing of our spirits and receive the healing of our bodies."

I would also add, "or the healing of our relationships." In so many words, Stanley Jones is emphasizing an age-old truth: "Forgiveness of sin and release from guilt are crucial in the healing process."

Ronald Meredith, author of one of my most treasured books, *Hurrin' Big for Little Reasons*, tells this story: One of his colts came up lame. Something was obviously wrong. The young animal could put no weight on one leg because of great pain. The vet came out to the little ranch and began to examine the colt's lame leg. Ron Meredith gently held the colt while the vet probed the hoof in search of whatever was causing the problem. When the hoof was cleaned, out there was every evidence of infection. The question remained as to the cause.

After almost an hour of searching, he found the trouble. "Here it is!" the doctor exclaimed. "I'll have it out in a minute."

Sure enough he did. Out of the colt's foot, he pulled a piece of rusty nail about three quarters of an inch in length. After cleaning the wound and giving the animal shots to keep down infection, the vet drove away from the ranch to his next call.

Ron Meredith, on the way back to the house, held the dirty little nail in his hand and studied it. A rusty nail has no place in a horses' foot. As long as it is there, there will be trouble.

There are things that don't belong in our lives, too. A soul can be festered by the presence of deeply embedded hate, fear, or an unforgiving spirit. Nails don't belong in a horse's foot. They must come out. Men and horses have much in common. Some things are just too costly to keep; an unforgiving spirit is one of them!

One of our scriptures tonight makes it abundantly clear just how important it is to live in the light of God's forgiveness.

> If we say we share in life with God and keep on living in the dark [committing intentional sins] we are lying and are not living by the truth. But if we live in the light, as God does, we share in life with each other. And the blood of his son washes all our sins away. [Jesus' death on the cross puts us right with God]. If we say that we have not sinned, we are fooling ourselves and the truth is not in our hearts. But if we confess our sins to God, He can always be trusted to forgive us and take our sins away. If we say that we have not sinned, we make God a liar and his message is not in our hearts.
> (I John 1:5-10, NRSV)

We also rejoice in the words of Psalm 103.

The Lord is merciful! He is kind and patient. His love never fails. The Lord won't always be angry and point out our sins. He doesn't punish us as our sins deserve. How great is Gods love for all who worship Him [that is, fear Him, stand in awe of Him, sincerely love Him]? Greater than the distance between heaven and earth. How far has the Lord taken our sins from us? Farther than the distance from East to West. Just as parents are kind to their children, the Lord is kind to all who worship him. (Psalm 103:8-13, NRSV)

When we truly worship God, putting Him and His ways first in our lives, we can be sure of His forgiveness. Not only that, but when we sincerely desire to please God, this desire in itself makes Him happy and pleases Him. It thrills God to forgive us and not hold our sins against us.

Looking at I John and Psalm 103, as we have, we begin to understand how important it is to God that we experience His forgiveness. So if, in fact, we are not feeling God's forgiveness and feeling better about ourselves, If our self-esteem is not where it should be, if our physical well being is not all that we desire, perhaps the fault lies more in ourselves than with God.

Two things are essential if forgiveness is to become realized. Forgiveness not just a word or an idea, but it is the result of these two things: (1) We must confess our sins to God. (2) We must be willing to forgive others.

In Matthew 18:21-35 is a story or parable about God's forgiveness being contingent upon our willingness and ability to forgive others. You may remember the parable is preceded by Peter asking Jesus how often he should forgive another member of the church who sins against him. In the Lord's Prayer, Jesus taught his closest followers the necessity of forgiving others. "Forgive us our sins (how?) as we have forgiven those who sin against us" (NRSV). So, this is one of the two essentials for forgiving others.

Let us think about the importance of confessing our own sins. Once again, we look to the psalmist:

The man who knows the meaning of forgiveness, whose past failures no longer plague him, who stands blameless and guilt free before God—that man is rich indeed. Every time I attempt to handle my own guilt by ignoring it, rationalizing it, or just running away from it—some unseen power of pressure from the depths of my being squeezes my life dry, leaving me empty. But when I face up to my failures and confess them, when I open my guilt-ridden heart to you, O God, then I realize the blessed meaning of forgiveness. (Psalm 32, *Leslie Brandi's Psalm Now,* v 1-3)

You and I have many opportunities to ask God for forgiveness. When we come to God in prayer during our daily quiet times, for one. Or every Sunday when we pray the Lord's Prayer. "Forgive us our sins as we forgive those who sin against us," we pray. Then we sit quietly as the offering is to be received. What better time, more opportune time than this to confess quietly to God one or two of those things that we have done the week before that we recognize as sinful.

If you and I want to experience the fullness of God's love we will find a time and a way to cleanse our minds and hearts through confession on a regular basis. We might begin by asking ourselves each night, "What have I done this day that I feel was pleasing to God? What have I done or said or thought this day that was displeasing to God."

Go to sleep thanking God for the blessings of the day and asking His forgiveness for the mistakes you have made. You will sleep better. It is interesting that in most prayer books or hymnals in many Denominations there are prayers of confession or contrition. The closest thing to such a prayer that I have found in our *Chalice Hymnal* is one entitled "A Prayer for Shedding Pretenses" (p 597). I have paraphrased it to make it more personal for myself. I hope you will find it helpful.

O God (who is all seeing and all knowing), you see through all false motives and hidden agendas. You look deeply into the silent, secret places and you see who we really are. You know all the places our true spirit dwells. Take away the desire we have to deceive you—those things we say and do that mask our real intentions. Forgive us for all of the ways we try to defend our misbehaviors and disguise who we really are. Help us O God to be open with you and honest with ourselves and others. Amen

If we can honestly pray something similar to this every night or each morning and live by it throughout the day, we will experience God's promised forgiveness, and we will be set free to live each moment to its fullest, and we will continue on the "road to wholeness."

Sharing God's Forgiveness
(Forgiving Others)

Forgiveness of sin and release from guilt are absolutely essential in the healing process—the process of becoming a whole person. Two things are crucial if forgiveness is to become the healing balm that God wants us to have. (1) We must confess our sins to God. (2) We must be willing to do so and actually forgive others. This second necessity is our focus tonight.

One of the first steps in being able to forgive someone who has deeply and unjustifiably hurt you, injured you, or tried to destroy you, is understanding. If you can sincerely try to recall all the circumstances surrounding the occasion of your being hurt, it will help you. I'll share with you a true story I first heard told by Doris Donnely.

A young mother while driving her old "clunker" of a car, with her three sons riding in the back seat, suddenly pulled over on the shoulder of the road, stopped, and reaching over the back of the front seat slapped the youngest of the three as hard as she could. The boys had all been arguing, but the mother took it all out on the youngest. The kid saw stars, his head hurt. Big tears began to roll down his cheeks.

The mother launched into a tirade of harsh words. "You! I hate you! The only reason I became pregnant and gave birth to you was to try to keep your no-good daddy from leaving me. But it didn't work. He's left us now!" (The little boy looked an awful lot like his daddy, almost a clone)

The mother continued to take all her frustrations out on the youngest boy while favoring the older two. It was grossly unfair to the youngest. He cried himself to sleep many nights—broken hearted.

Finally, he reached age eighteen and left home. Eventually, he met a wonderful Christian girl, fell in love, married, and became active in her church. More and more, he longed for reconciliation with his mother who was in her forties by now. He located her, contacted her, and asked if he could come to see her. She consented.

Upon arriving, he entered her little home with some degree of uneasiness. The last thing he wanted to do was cause any more hurt to his mother or to himself.

He began by saying, "Mama, I have given much thought as to why you acted toward me as you did twenty years ago. You were young with four mouths to feed. Your old car could have quit running at any time. You had no one to hold you or encourage you. I see it all, now, Mama. I have prayed many times that God would help me make sense of it all, and He has. Mama, I love you. I thank you for bringing me into the world and providing for me with food, clothing, and shelter. I love you."

By this time, the mother was sobbing so hard her shoulders were shaking. They reached out to each other, embraced, and held on, both crying so hard that they could hardly breathe. Tears of regret became tears of joy. Their mutual forgiveness became reconciliation. Reconciliation became freedom and joy and hope.

What a blessing for mother and son! Reconciliation occurred in this situation because both of them desired it, wanted it, longed for it. Reconciliation is the restoring of a harmonious relationship between two or more people. It is a beautiful experience, bringing a measure of peace, hope, and wholeness where hatred, hurt, and brokenness had existed.

This brings us to the question: "Can I forgive others without reconciliation occurring?" The answer is yes! You can forgive a person who doesn't know she has hurt you. You can forgive a parent or grandparent who is no longer present on this earth. We can forgive persons or groups of persons without their consciously knowing it or having any way to respond.

This "one-way" forgiveness is a matter of releasing others from the harsh judgment in our own hearts. This forgiveness brings a measure of peace even if the other person does not or cannot, for whatever reason, forgive us or even ask for our forgiveness. Therefore, even a one-way forgiveness is crucial to our becoming a whole person.

However, we can refuse to forgive others. When we do, our reluctance to extend forgiveness holds us captive. When we refuse to forgive, we hold others firmly enmeshed in the bondage of our judgment. It binds us to the past, imprisons us. It impedes the present moment and the future potential of life. A refusal to forgive holds us captive just as much as it does the other person.

In the Lord's Prayer we pray, "Forgive us our debts as we forgive our debtors," or "Forgive us our sins as we forgive those who sin against us." This verse of scripture (Matthew 6:12) has also been translated, "Loose the cords of mistakes binding us, as we release the strands we hold of others guilt," or "Lighten our load of secret debts as we relieve others of their need to repay," or "Forgive our hidden past, the secret shames, as we consistently forgive what others hide."

Looking at forgiveness this way we recognize it as a gift that we can give one another, an opportunity to let go of the mistakes that tie ourselves and one another in knots. It is this entanglement of emotions and hard feelings—this feeling of being tied in knots with someone—that makes forgiveness an experience of liberation for both parties. Seeing forgiveness in this light should encourage us to want to forgive.

It is interesting that Matthew 18:18 takes on a deeper meaning when we apply it to forgiveness. Jesus told Peter and other disciples, "Whatever you bind on earth will be bound in heaven" (NRSV). If we insist on remaining bound to someone in resentment, heaven will not force us to change our minds. If we remain unwilling to forgive those who wound us, hurt us deeply, how can God set us free from the entanglement of a broken relationship?

God wants more than anything else for us to be set free, to experience wholeness and oneness with Him. This is why "the Word became flesh and dwelt among us, full of grace and truth" (John 1:14-15, NRSV), to give us a way out of brokenness, heartache and entanglement. But if we refuse to pass the gift of grace to others who have "sinned against us," we prevent the grace of God's forgiveness from entering our own lives in all its fullness. Then what is "bound on earth remains bound in heaven," not by God's design, but by our own. An unforgiving heart blocks the mystery of divine grace. It cannot receive what God freely gives.

How can it happen? Real forgiveness is not humanly possible. We need God's grace to help us. Forced forgiveness is not what we are talking about here. Authentic forgiveness flows freely from the heart. How do we experience a change of heart? The cry of the

15

psalmist must be our cry. "Create in me a clean heart, O God" (Psalm 51:10, NRSV). We remain helpless to forgive out of our own ego-strength. However, following an earnest prayer for God's help, we might benefit from some practical steps in the process of forgiveness. Doris Donnely identifies these steps as follows:

- **Acknowledge the hurt or pain you are feeling:** Swallow your pride. Admit you have been hurt by someone's thoughtlessness, criticism, rejection, neglect, or ingratitude.
- **Make a conscious decision to forgive:** Forgiveness is an act of the will. I will do this! I "will" to forgive this person. At this point, you do not need to know how you are going to do it or when you are going to do it. You don't need a precise strategy—just the firm conviction, "This is what I will do—I will forgive!"
- **Remember forgiveness is a process:** It will take time. You are dealing with hurt and brokenness. A broken arm or leg takes time to heal. A broken relationship is no different.
- **Remember forgiveness is not easy:** It is not natural, it is supernatural, and requires God's grace. In this respect, God must be involved because true forgiveness always involves death, a little death. Death is not easy or pleasant to endure, even the death of pride!
- **Immerse yourself in autobiographical writings:** Read testimonies of others who have been there and know what you are going through, such as Abraham Lincoln, Corrie Ten Boom and others. Find out how they moved from hopelessness to wholeness.
- **Forgive yourself:** Whatever your role in the broken relationship might be, remember that one experience is just a part of you. Another person's forgiveness can be real to you only when you forgive yourself of any part you played in the brokenness.
- **Try to see the one who hurt you in a new light:** Try to understand the circumstances in his/her life at the time of the injury. What role did fear, lack of information, insecurity or ignorance play in that event? What unhealed hurts in their past or your past contributed to the breech in relationship?

I close this homily with one more true story. John Claypool first told this story.

A merchant somewhere in the Midwest had identical twin sons. These boy's lives were inseparably intertwined. From earliest years, they dressed alike, went to the same schools and colleges. In fact, they were so close that neither of them ever married.

After finishing their college degrees, they returned to work with their dad. When he died, they took over the business. The community looked up to them. Their relationship was pointed to as a model of creative collaboration in the retail business.

One morning a customer came into the store and made a small purchase. The brother who waited on him put two dollar bills on top of the cash register and walked to the front door with the customer in friendly conversation.

Sometime later, he remembered what he had done, returned to the cash register and found the dollar bills gone. He asked his brother if he had seen the bills and perhaps put them in the register, and his brother replied that "he knew nothing about the money in question."

"That's funny; I distinctly remember placing it there on the register, and no one else has been in the store since then."

Had the matter been dropped at that point, a mystery involving a tiny amount of money, nothing would have come of it. However, an hour later, this time with a noticeable hint of suspicion in his voice, the brother asked again, "Are you sure you didn't see those dollar bills?"

The other brother was quick to catch the note of accusation, and flared back in defensive anger. This unusual exchange of words was the first serious breach of trust that had ever come between these two. It grew wider and deeper. Every time they tried to discuss the issue, new charges and countercharges were added, until finally things got so bad that they were forced to dissolve the partnership.

They built a partition—a wall—down the middle of their father's store and turned what had been a harmonious partnership into an angry competition. In fact, that business became a source of division in the entire community, each twin trying to enlist allies for himself against the other. This open warfare went on for over twenty years.

Then one day, a car with out of state license plates drove up in front of the store. A well-dressed man got out and went into one side of the store and inquired how long the merchant had been in business at that location. When he learned it had been over twenty years, the stranger said, "Then you are the one with whom I must settle an old, old account."

"Some twenty years ago, I was out of work, drifting from place to place, and I happened to get off a railroad box car in your town. I had absolutely no money. I had not eaten for three days. As I was walking down the alley behind your store, I looked in and saw two dollar bills on top of the cash register. Everyone else was in the front of the store. I had been raised in a Christian home and had never stolen anything. That morning, though, I was so hungry I gave in to the temptation, walked quietly through the back door, and took the dollar bills."

"What I did has haunted me all these years, and I finally decided I would never be at peace until I came back and faced up to my sin. Would you allow me to pay you back plus whatever interest or damages you feel appropriate?"

The old man, that one twin, began to shake his head in dismay. Big tears ran down his cheeks. When he finally got control of his emotions, he took the stranger by the arm and said, "Would you please go next door and tell that man over there what you just told me?"

The stranger did that, only this time there were two old men who looked remarkably alike standing before him and weeping uncontrollably.

To think—twenty years of hostility, hatred, and destruction, and it all rooted back to a spirit of mistrust that came to exist between them, a mistrust that, tragically enough, had no basis in reality at all.

Could this be true in our lives at times? Following Christ Jesus, denying ourselves requires trust—trust in Christ, trust in ourselves, and a willingness to forgive when things go wrong.

Forgiveness touches everyone's life. Forgiveness is the difference between hope or despair, love or hatred.

All Things Work Together . . .
Romans 8:18, 28 38-39

To become a whole person, faith is absolutely essential. On many occasions, Jesus said to men and women, "Your faith has made you well. Your faith has healed you. Your faith has made you whole."

I want us to reflect on ways in which we deepen our faith, believing as we do that God is still in control of our lives as well as the universe.

God speaks to us in all kinds of events and happenings, even though we may not be aware of him speaking to us or even aware that God is present. There are, of course, some moments, some events, some happenings that trigger our awareness, acutely or keenly, that God is here, now. A beautiful sunrise or sunset, a newborn baby, flowers and trees bursting forth in all their splendor, an anthem sung by our choir, a solo that has touched us in some special way. We all identify with these happenings as things that strengthen our faith, our trust in God.

We all know, however, that these beautiful, inspiring, uplifting events are not the only things that take place in our lives. We learn early on in life that bad things happen to good people. A bully confronts us while we are still in our childhood at school, pushing us around, using us, and abusing us. As teenagers, many people experience the pain that accompanies having lies told about them. Jealousy triggers gossip, lies, and mental abuse. On the job or even at church, we encounter individuals who work from hidden agendas to position themselves so that, always, they must win or come out on top, regardless of how unfair or even unscrupulous their actions and behaviors may be. A person who never smoked may come down with lung cancer. A person who never consumed alcohol may find that he or she has been diagnosed with cirrhosis of the liver. The list could go on and on.

We know the truth of the saying, "life is not fair." I don't know of any place in Jesus' teaching where He said or taught that life will always be fair. Sooner or later, we discover that the finest, most upright, God-fearing people go through difficult times or adversities.

What Jesus does teach us is this: God is always with us. Jesus said fear not, for I am with you. "A tiny bird, a sparrow, is not of much value by worldly standards. Yet God does not forget a single one of them. Are you not of more value than a whole flock of sparrows?" (Luke 12: 4-7, NRSV).

In becoming a whole person in Christ, we will face up to the fact that life is not always easy. Life is not always fair. Bad things do happened to good people.

Recently Dot and I had the privilege of visiting with one of our congregation's most interesting and inspiring members. A man who, in spite of many obstacles, has remained a whole person in Christ, His spirit has sustained him through many difficult times, through the thick and thin and ups and down of life.

Dot asked him, "Charles, tell us how you have been able to keep your faith in spite of all you have been through."

This man has suffered from diabetes for twenty-one years. He was declared legally blind several years ago. For a number of years now, he has spent four or five hours a day on dialysis three times a week. He has undergone surgery several times and because of poor circulation had to give up portions of both lower limbs.

So during our visit (a visit with Charles is always a blessing), Dot said, "Charles, your spirit, your countenance, your witness has been such a positive influence on many people. Your whole life, your deep faith has helped so many of us. Tell us, how have you kept this inner light shining so brightly?"

Charles responded, "To put it real simple, it has been my daily walk in faith with the Lord, knowing that He is in complete control at all times. Some things that we wouldn't like to see happen do, in fact, happen. There must be some reason for it. We may not know today what that reason is, but we do know that God is with us. A person cannot control some things that happen to him or her, but they can control their attitude about what happens."

Charles Cork is a shining example of how one can remain a whole person in Christ regardless of circumstances and physical conditions. We can learn from him, benefit from his life.

But, to fully understand we must know and remember some of the positive influences in his life. He was born in 1935. His maternal grandmother, a Godly woman lived with his family. She read her Bible many hours each day. Charles took note of that.

Even today when he reflects on her life and her influence, his voice takes on a tender tone as in his mind he must see her, sitting there in her rocking chair, hour-by-hour, feeding on God's word, becoming a whole person herself.

It is also important to know that Charles' father prayed earnestly to be delivered from a heavy addiction to cigarettes. Charles' father was a chain smoker. You know the kind. You've seen them. You can recall the particulars: fingers and teeth yellowed by nicotine. The constant anxiety or concern, "Do I have enough cigarettes to last until I get back to the store?"

The older Mr. Cork knew he had to give it all up. He prayed sincerely believingm and God did not fail him. God did not let him down. Charles said, "Daddy quit without any difficulty whatsoever." This evidence of God's unfailing love made a lasting impression on the boy who grew up to be a man of deep faith.

Today, in spite of being visually handicapped, in spite of dialysis, in spite of both legs being amputated just below the knees, yes, and in spite of bedsores, Charles Cork is a whole person, because of his spirit, his faith in God. All of this reminds us that we do not have to be in perfect physical condition to be a whole person!

A whole lot depends on how we view our limitations. Charles Cork said, "Some things happen that we would very much not like to see happen. A person cannot control everything that happens. But a person can control his or her attitude about what happens."

God puts people in our lives to help us become a whole person—a parent, a grandparent or a Christian friend. Let us never fail to thank God for those people. We all live through crises in our lives. If we can remain focused on some eternal truths, we will come through victoriously.

The apostle Paul was a model for us. He suffered shipwreck, imprisonment, beatings, and persecution, yet his faith remained strong. He said, "You know, the things that we are suffering now cannot be compared with the glory about to be revealed to us. There is no comparison between the present hard times and the good times coming" (Romans 8:18, NRSV).

"We know that all things work together for good for those who Love God. We can be sure that every detail in our lives will be worked into something good!" (Romans 8:28, NRSV).

21

"For I am convinced that neither death, nor life, nor angels, or rulers, nor things present, nor things to come, nor powers, nor height, nor depth, nor anything in all creation, will be able to separate us from the love of God in Christ Jesus our Lord.

"Nothing living or dead, angelic or demonic, today or tomorrow, high or low, thinkable or unthinkable, absolutely nothing can get between us and God's love because of the way that Jesus, our Master has embraced us." (Romans 8:38-39 NRSV/The Message)

A deep and abiding faith in God helps us to remember that, in spite of outward appearances, God is still in control. Deep within history as we know it, the history that gets written down in history books, newspapers, and magazines, there flows a sacred history, God's ultimate purpose being worked out in the human history that has no apparent meaning or purpose. This is the faith that sustained the Israelites, God's chosen people. Chosen to suffer—suffer and remain faithful as a witness to Yahweh, the one true God. The only reason they were chosen was not because they were special in any other way, but because of their faith in the sovereignty and power of God.

But the reality of sacred history is important. Ask those God fearing people in all centuries who have been persecuted because of their beliefs. Ask people, good people like Charles Cork, who have lived through one horrible health problem after another never giving up hope. They will tell you that "nothing will get between me and God's love because of the way that Jesus my Master embraces me daily."

Ask a young woman in Missouri who has survived a living hell due to the cruelty inflicted on her by one she loved and trusted. She will tell you about sacred history and faith needed to hold on and keep trusting God. Know that God is still in the picture. Ask yourself. Ask the writer of Psalm 13.

> How much longer, Lord, will you forget about me? Will it be forever? How long will you hide? How long must I be confused and miserable all day? Please listen, Lord God, make my eyes sparkle again or else I will fall...(In the past) I trusted your love; your steadfast love; my heart shall rejoice

in your salutation. I will sing to the Lord because you rescued me. You have been good to me. (NRSV)

Here, we have one of the "Psalms of Lament." In these Psalms, we find the Psalmist grieving or mourning over his misfortune for the first part of the Psalm. But then his recall, his memory kicks in, and he is aware of God's goodness, God's blessings in former times. The writer of the Psalms, the prayer book of the Bible, knew all about sacred history, salvation history.

Wherever you may be in your journey toward wholeness, if you can sincerely believe that God is in the picture working for your good because He loves you, you are on the right path.

> Wholeness means living creatively within our own limitations, not wasting our days in envy at the capacities and capabilities of others, not despairing at the loss of youth and vigor or at the lack of maturity and experience, not giving up when our best efforts produce far less than we had hoped for, not torturing ourselves with guilt when having to settle for the lesser of two evils. For to be fully alive is to be whole, fully alive here and now just as things are, not yet in the fullness of God's kingdom which remains in the future. In the meantime, we are called to live the life of faith in a world that is still far less than it ought to be, far short of what God intends. (Norman Young, *Healing, Wholeness and the Mystery of Grace*, Lecture, 1985, Australia)

Prayer

Lord God,

Keeper of our souls, healer of our minds, our bodies, our spirits and our relationships, we praise you that you have given us eyes of faith so that we can perceive that you are in fact working out your ultimate purpose for creation including our individual lives. Help us to remember that your "eye is on the Sparrow." Help us to know that you are watching over and caring for us day by day, minute by minute.

In the name of our Great Physician, Your Son, Our Lord and Savior.

Amen

He Touched Me
Matthew 8:1-3 Psalm 103: 1 - 3

On page 564 in our Chalice Hymnal, we find the words of a song that has blessed many souls since 1963 when Bill Gaither penned them. It is a song that expresses the joy that fills a soul of a person made whole by the great physician, Jesus Christ.

> *Since I met this blessed savior,*
> *since He cleansed and made me whole,*
> *I will never cease to praise him.*
> *I'll shout it while eternity rolls.*
> *He touched me; O He touched me,*
> *and O the joy that floods my soul!*
> *Something happened, and now I know,*
> *He touched me and made me whole.*

Consider also this hymn:

> *Surely the presence of the Lord is in this place.*
> *I can feel His mighty power and His grace.*
> *I can hear the brush of angel's wings;*
> *I see glory on each face.*
> *Surely the presence of the Lord is in this place.*

These two praise hymns, gospel songs, portray the essence of what we, the healing team, hope for, pray for and long for every time we worship.

In our first scripture tonight, we learned of a great crowd following Jesus. Among that crowd was a leper, a man disfigured by the most horrible disease of that day. The man came to Jesus, knelt before Him, and said, "Lord if you choose, you can make me clean." Jesus stretched out his hand, touched him, saying, "I do choose, be made clean!" Immediately his leprosy was cleansed.

Can you use your imagination a bit? Can you see and hear the man healed from leprosy clapping his hands and shouting, *"something happened, and now I know, He touched me and made me whole."* Can you see and hear this celebration? I can! What a gift, a man dancing, shouting and praising God.

In our second scripture, we learn about Simon Peter's mother-in-law lying in bed with a fever. Jesus touched her hand and the fever left her. She got up immediately and began to serve Him.

Now, go a step further in your imagination with me. Can you enter Simon Peter's house and witness this dear woman with a high fever, covered with blankets because of chills and shivering? Only her hand is exposed from under the covers. Jesus gently touches her hand with His hand and—poof! The fever is gone!

This woman, probably in her late 50's to early 60's throws the covers back, gets up, and begins to serve her son-in-law and others in the house, but especially Jesus. I can see her putting food on the table, lifting her eyes and her voice in praise. Why, I can even here this woman singing, *"He touched me; O He touched me, and O the joy that floods my soul. Something happened, and now I know, He touched me and made me whole."* Jesus is still touching people and making them whole.

Go with me now to the year 1980. A fifty-three-year-old man, "burning the candle at both ends"—something he had been doing for too many years: working two jobs, going to graduate school, feeling tired, losing weight, pushing, trying to do far too much on his own strength, loving his family dearly, but never seeming to have enough time to do all he wanted to do, especially with those he loved most dearly. If a person was ever on the brink of total burnout, it wan this man.

In March of 1981, a severe, intense pain in the lower left abdomen prompted a visit to his primary physician, admittance to the hospital, and x-rays. A very suspicious cloud or dark area in his colon was seen. Test were prescribed: a sigmodiscope, but to no avail. Total blockage of the colon prevented a successful scoping. Surgery was performed by a renowned surgeon who performed intestinal and colon surgery every week.

In the operating room: a removal of thirteen inches of diseased tissue from the colon, a quick-freeze of the tissue, an "it doesn't look good," a call from surgery to patient's room.

"Mrs. Goodwin, I'm afraid I don't have good news. Every indication is that your husband has cancer. We removed a section of diseased and perforated colon, and we cleaned the other tissue to which it was attached. We removed some lymph nodes. I'll have a complete report in a day or so."

26

There was shock, disbelief, tears, and prayers—many, many prayers by family, friends local and long distance, and several congregations.

During the regular worship service being broadcast over radio, Lindenwood's senior minister asked for prayers for his long-time friend. Strangers listening in began to pray. The most intense prayers were lifted by the man's wife and sweetheart of thirty-seven years (at that time).

God placed in her mind and broken heart these words: "Are any among you sick? They should call for the elders of the church and have them pray over them, anointing them with oil in the name of the Lord. The prayer of faith will save the sick, and the Lord will raise them up..." (James 5:13-15a, NRSV).

This dear, brokenhearted wife called her church's chairman of elders and requested just such prayer. She was told, "we're all praying night and day."

She said, "I know that, but God has spoken to me and told me to ask for the elders to come with oil and anoint my husband and pray for healing."

The chairman said, "Let me talk to the elders, and I'll get back with you."

In the mean time, on Saturday night, the sick man's brother, a timid soul in one sense, came to the hospital, room 462 Methodist North. He said to the sick man, "Little brother, I'm here to pray with you. I've brought some olive oil and I'm gonna do what we're told to do in the book of James." Together the sick man's wife and brother prayed earnestly that God would heal their loved one.

The next day, Sunday, this man's dear wife placed her hand gently over her husband's abdomen, envisioned God's healing power at work healing any diseased tissue that may not have been removed.

Late that afternoon, when other family members were gone, she sat by his bed holding his hand, touching his abdomen ever so lightly at times. A soft rain was caressing the outside of the windowpane, and something happened. The room was filled by peace, a peace that was felt by a sick man and his loving wife. A peace like they had never felt before. Everything was going to be all right. All fear was gone, all doubt removed. That evening, they watched and listened to an evangelical worship service on

27

television. The scripture that appeared on the screen was the third scripture read to you tonight, Psalm 103: 1-3 "Bless the Lord, O my soul, and all that is within me, bless His holy name. Bless the Lord, O my soul, and do not forget all His benefits, who forgives all your sins and heals all your diseases" (NRSV). Was that a coincidence? I think not!

Friday and Saturday had been difficult days. Saturday night and Sunday brought hope and joy, even before the surgeon called on the phone Monday to say, "Mrs. Goodwin, I have good news."

"Praise God!" she interrupted, "it's not in the lymph nodes."

The doctor spoke again. "No. It is not in the lymph nodes. Mrs. Goodwin, I do this surgery almost every week, sometimes two or three times in a week. I know what malignant tissue cuts like and looks like. I can even detect a certain odor with it at times. All the bad signs were there when I called you from surgery on Friday.

"I apologize for being so long getting back to you. Part of the reason is this: I was so sure it was cancer, I didn't want to give you a conflicting good report unless I was 100% sure. So, I had the pathology department downtown do a second workup. Whatever was there in the operating room on Friday is no longer there."

This telephone call was followed by tears of joy and prayers of praise!

It just so happened that the elders arrived in the downstairs lobby shortly after the good news came. They came on up to the room and together they lifted their voices with the man and his wife.

"God is so good, God is so good, God is so good! He's so good to me. He answers prayer, He answers prayer, He answers prayer. He's so good to me!" Ten or twelve voices sang with joy.

One of the nurses at the desk came hurrying to the room. "Shhh!" she said. "That's much too much noise in a hospital, you'll make me lose my job! Are you folk charismatic? Are you Pentecostal?"

The sick man spoke up. "Yes ma'am, at a time like this we are really Pentecostal, if by that you mean exuberant with joy. We're really Pentecostal."

Tuesday morning a young nurse who lived in Fayette County had come back to work after being off for a long weekend. She heard the good news, came running into the room hugging and crying.

She said, "you know, I went home Friday night worn out, considering giving up nursing. But not now! My faith is restored."

Around noon Tuesday, or shortly thereafter, another surgeon came to the room. "I was in surgery on Friday with your husband assisting Dr. Birdsong through the surgery. I was so pleased to hear the good report. What have you folk been doing?"

The wife answered, "Praying. Praying and praising!"

"Keep it up, said the doctor. That is the best prescription I know." He left the room with a big smile on his face.

"Something happened and now I know, He touched me and made me whole."

Something happens when we pray that would not happen had we not prayed. The sincere prayers of a righteous person availeth much. There is great celebration in heaven when a child of God is healed, made whole, spiritually or mentally or physically or when a broken relationship is healed and restored.

I can tell you there was great celebration at Methodist north hospital April 24, 1981. This couple had moved through apprehension, anxiety, deep concern, disappointment, depression, pain, and disbelief to a time of surrender, trust, hope, peace, and exuberant praise and thanksgiving.

"Something happened and now I know, He touched me and made me whole."

Once again, we are faced with a great mystery. Why is it some prayers for healing seem to be answered while others are not? During our very first time together in this ministry of Praise, Prayer, Holy Communion, and Healing, we said frankly it is a futile effort to try to find an answer as to why some are healed and others are not.

Shortly after the healing experience just shared took place, a wonderful Christian woman was diagnosed with cancer and died within a year. She was much needed by her elderly mother. She was a dear, dear friend of the couple who celebrated a healing on April 24, 1981. It was a mystery then and it remains a mystery today. Much of what happens here will remain a mystery until we are united with our God face to face.

29

This does not deter us or discourage us in our ministry of healing. We wouldn't even be asking why some are not healed if we had not witnessed and been persuaded that some are healed. Not even modern medicine and surgery results in universal success. "Can you take penicillin?" asks the nurse or physician. They know that for some people, penicillin—medical therapy—is not effective, but counterproductive. Why should we expect that prayer for healing—spiritual therapy—will be effective with everyone for whom we pray? The teachings and prayers of Jesus failed to make Judas a whole person. The faith that healed many people throughout Palestine healed only a few sick folk in Jesus' hometown.

In spite of the many factors involved, we go on believing with all our hearts and minds that Jesus is the Great Physician, and He does have the power to heal. We will go on believing that Christ cares for us. If something is hurting us, causing distress or disease, Jesus cares about that. He desires to help us, to touch us, and make us whole.

Celebrate with the man cured of leprosy. Celebrate with Simon Peter's mother-in-law. Celebrate with a man healed of cancer in 1981.

He touches us and makes us whole so that we will have renewed physical energy for serving Him and our fellow human beings. So let us pray for ourselves and for others. We are all connected through faith in God. One human being can lift up another human being to God's healing love. The prayers—sincere, fervent prayers—of a wife or a brother, a sister or a mother, can enrich the healing process in ones life. This is our faith! This is our reason for being here tonight.

Prayer

Loving God,

Hear the praise and thanksgiving of one who was healed not because of anything he did, but because of the loving concern and prayers of a devout wife and three children and a multitude of friends and even some strangers. You touched me, o you touched me, and a joy still fills my soul. Something happened, and now I know, You touched me and made me whole."

Christ Can Set Us Free
Luke 4:18-19

Suppose someone spoke to you saying, "Good news! Christ can set you free!" What would be your response? "Really? I didn't know I was in bondage," or "I'm not in jail, or under house arrest. I'm not shackled or hand cuffed. I live in a free nation, thank God."

These and other such reactions might well be our immediate responses. If we give some thought and contemplation to that statement, however, we might realize that most, if not all, human beings find themselves in some kind of bondage at some time: fear or anxiety, panic attacks, old resentments that keep coming back, a persistent lack of self confidence... All of these, to say nothing of addictions such as tobacco, alcohol, prescription drug abuse, gossip, lying, profanity, etc.

Very few people, including avowed Christians—even church leaders, are totally free from attitudes and actions that limit their abilities and their Christian influence. It may be just a persistent negative outlook on life that can lead to cynicism.

In light of all the unscrupulous behavior and evil in our society and culture today—world politics, national politics, even church politics at times—it could be easy to become a real cynic. A cynic is a person who believes that most, if not all, people are motivated out of total selfishness.

Do you ever find yourself tempted to turn off the TV, discontinue the newspaper, and just withdraw from the world for a while? This may not be the courageous Christian thing to do. We are reminded by scripture that we cannot escape living in the world, but we are not to be conformed by the world, either. (Romans 12:2, NRSV)

Jesus can set us free from anything—any attitude, mind set, life style, or habit—that would put us in bondage, keeping us from being the whole, happy, healthy persons God created us to be.

On pages 128-132 in a book, *The Unlimited Power of Prayer*, published by Guideposts, William Wilson, a professor of Psychiatry at Duke University, tells a story of how his life took on new meaning and purpose because of a weeklong scouting trip in the wilds of Minnesota. He was, in a sense, set free from the bondage of life becoming a drag. He was set free by God.

Before he went on that trip with his oldest son he was tired, worn out. Late one afternoon, about 7:00, one of his colleagues on faculty at Duke stopped by his desk.

"Bill," he said, "got a minute?"

"Sure," said Dr. Wilson, "what's up?"

"Well," said his friend, "my life is a drag. I don't understand it. I mean, you'd think I have everything. I'm a full professor here at the university. I have unlimited access to a huge laboratory, research facilities, and library. Journals publish my papers. The government awards me grants. I've got a great wife and nice kids. So why do I feel so empty inside?"

Bill Wilson wished he could give his friend an answer that would offer real hope. But all he could say was, "The way you're feeling isn't unusual. If it's any consolation, I often feel the same way."

This brief conversation left him feeling vaguely depressed. He wondered why. Perhaps he was just tired, working too hard, fatigued. He hurried home thinking about his upcoming eight-day scouting trip with his son. In the next few weeks, he jogged and did sit-ups to get in shape.

"You know Dad," commented his son, "I think you're looking forward to this trip as much as I am." (His son was right.)

Bill Wilson, as a boy, had spent many days hunting, fishing, and exploring the wonders of the woods of North Carolina. Although he had not been a religious person, even as a boy, he had found those quiet times in the forest to be very special. So, he was indeed looking forward to the trip.

The scout leader was a college aged youth, tall, muscular with copper colored hair and beard. The young leader took a liking to those he was leading, especially Bill Wilson and his son. He led the group with unlimited energy and enthusiasm. It was an unforgettable trip!

The seventh day of the trip was a Sunday. According to scout rules, a brief outdoor worship service was called for. The young leader, stood atop a large boulder and gave a little talk based on Matthew 23:26. "Blind Pharisee, first clean the inside of the cup, so that the outside also may become clean" (NRSV). He went on to compare the wilderness, in all its splendor and untouched beauty, to the way the inside of our lives ought to be. Then the group was led in a sing-along of simple Gospel songs. Their voices rang out pure and clear in the cool morning air.

As Bill Wilson listened to those sounds, he suddenly felt something, some untapped emotional stirring deep inside of himself. It had been a long time since he had even thought about God.

That evening, as the sun was setting, he walked to the edge of Basswood Lake, immense and sparkling beneath a pastel colored sky. He kicked off his moccasins and let his toes play along the pebbles on the shore. His thoughts returned to that morning, the simple worship service, and the strange effect it had on him.

He was a man of science in a field where all religions were often looked upon with real skepticism. The idea of a living God had always seemed remote and archaic to him. But there was nothing outdated about what he had heard in the message that morning: "God wanted us to be clean and healthy inside as well as outside, in order to be the kind of human beings he had created us to be." Inherent in that concept, pure and simple, was the essence of modern psychiatry.

It suddenly became apparent to Bill Wilson that the only true way to clean up your life and experience fulfillment wasn't through science, wasn't through medicine, and wasn't through psychiatry. It was through God. And looking out over those placid waters, Bill Wilson knew that was what he wanted and needed more than anything in the world—for God to come into his life and make him whole.

Tears streamed down his face. The sunset melted into a golden blur. He was overwhelmed, flooded with God's love. God was truly with Bill Wilson. His presence filled him with a peace and reassurance he'd never before known. "I savored the experience as long as I could," he said, "but then it was time to go."

That night, as the group paddled their canoes in the moonlight, Wilson remained silent, lost in thought about what had happened. He knew he had changed.

When he got home, it seemed he loved his wife more deeply and was more tolerant and kind with the kids. He found himself going back to church. He actually wanted to go. He met new friends at church. The fellowship there nurtured his newfound faith.

At work, however, Bill had to use some discretion. The prevailing attitude was generally negative where religion was concerned. There was, of course, good reason. The doctors where Wilson worked could remember a deranged old man who thought he was the prophet Jeremiah, and others who had complicated their mental and emotional problems with self-imposed guilt due to their misunderstanding of scriptures.

In fact, there was a rule that incoming psychiatric patients were not allowed to have Bibles. At one time, these professional attitudes seemed logical to Wilson, but now, he knew without a doubt that God was helping him in his own personal life. Why, he wondered, couldn't God do the same for his patients? He prayed asking God to lead him. Soon he was allowing patients to have their Bibles. He was willing to let his patients discuss their faith with him, to talk religion with him. In his own words, Dr. Wilson said, "The Lord was leading me slowly, no faster than I could handle, to the appropriate people and situations."

In the article he wrote for *Guideposts*, he concludes with the true story of a young man, a drug addicted physician who, when admitted to the hospital, was taking up to 40 tranquilizers a day, a paper cupful of pills. After two months of treatment and no discernible progress, Dr. Wilson had to say to him, "There is really nothing more I can do."

"Please," begged the patient, "please don't say that. I'm standing here craving drugs just as badly as the day I checked in here. Please, there's got to be something else."

Dr. Wilson called him by name and said, "There's nothing else I can do, but maybe there's something God can do."

"God?" whispered the man with a glimmer of hope in his voice.

"Yes," said Wilson, "God."

Suddenly, Wilson remembered the day his colleague, his good friend had stopped by his office saying, "Why is my life such a drag? Why do I feel so empty inside?" And Wilson had nothing to offer. Since returning from the scouting trip, Wilson had promised himself he would never let that happen again. He had never shared his experience at Basswood Lake and the moonlit canoe trip with anyone. But now, he told this young drug addicted physician his whole story. The young man listened intently. Wilson concluded by saying, "My advice is simply this, pray. Get down on your knees and pray. And don't get up until you've felt God in your life. He's waiting for you, and He wants to help." With these words Dr. Wilson left the patient. It was the end of another long day.

The next morning, Wilson looked in on the patient who returned his eye contact with eyes as clear and untroubled as the waters of Basswood Lake. So remarkable was this change that Dr. Wilson was able to send him home after only three additional days of observation.

Prayer remained one of Dr. Wilson's most effective tools in psychiatric treatment and counseling. God, through his miraculous power, touched Dr. William Wilson.

God can touch you and me and free us from any bondage we face. It may not be 40 tranquilizers or alcoholism, but whatever it is that's keeping you from experiencing fullness of life God can touch your life and set you free to become all He created you to be.

What a powerful, true story by a humble but courageous psychiatrist. There are several lessons to be learned:

> 1. If we are honest, open, and humble with God, God can come to us in the most unexpected ways: a scouting trip, a quiet night under the stars, a moment of reflection, sitting in the presence of a friend, in the throes of confusion and chaos, or in the midst of great doubt or deep depression. If we will do the very best we can to remain honest with ourselves and honest with God, the living Christ can enter our lives and set us free. Jesus said, "You shall know the truth, and the truth will set you free" (John 8:32, NRSV).

> 2. It is not always easy or comfortable to follow what you know to be the truth. Dr. Wilson had to remain open. Once he was back at work, he allowed the Lord to lead him slowly to the right people and the appropriate situations. He had faith in God. He trusted God to lead him, one step at a time.

> 3. Remaining open and honest with God and with ourselves will open doors of opportunity we never dreamed possible. Because Dr. Wilson had the courage to pray regularly for

every person in his care, before and after sessions, because he prayed silently during his conversations with patients, the power of God never ceased to amaze him. That power did not go unnoticed by others.

The news of his success with theretofore-hopeless cases like the young drug addicted physician spread rapidly. Professional organizations began calling on Dr. Wilson to speak on the subject of Christian Psychiatry at their meetings. Not long afterwards he began to offer a course called Christianity in Medicine and Psychiatry.

If Christ has set you free from some form of bondage and you are willing to honestly, yet humbly, share that with others, there is no limit to how God can use you.

4. Remember that in spite of all the unscrupulous behavior and evil that is in our world, there is still a lot of good, a lot that is right and Christ like. Take Paul's words to heart, "Whatever is good and pure and wholesome, think on these things."

So in summary do these things:

1. Remain open.
2. Trust God to lead you thru difficulties.
3. Share your faith with others.
4. Fill your mind with the good things around you.

Prayer

God, we come surrendering and relinquishing whatever it is in our lives that keeps us from being truly free. We come to leave at the table and at the foot of the cross anything, absolutely anything, large or small, that would keep us in bondage of any kind.

We love you, and we sense your great love for us. We are thrilled that you save us from a world that is imperfect and you empower us to help make it a better world. You save us from ourselves. We turn loose of anything and everything that is negative and non-positive.

In the powerful and power filled name of Jesus, we pray.

Amen

Spiritual IV's
Psalm 66: 1, 2, 16-20

"A Worship Service of Praise, Prayer, Holy Communion, and Healing!" It is our belief, our faith that each of the first three elements in this title contributes to the fourth. Healing occurs when we come here to worship. It is in part due to our praising God, our praying, and our partaking of Holy Communion.

Tonight, we will give our primary attention to prayer and the role it plays in the healing process. Sometimes you hear someone say, "We've done everything we know to do. All we can do now is pray." A physician or nurse may say something similar. "It's all in God's hands now," as if it wasn't in God's hands from the beginning.

Unfortunately, even devout Christians may look upon prayer as a last resort, rather than one of our primary resources in combating illness or coping with personal problems. Let us never forget this: prayer is one of our primary resources.

As James K. Wagner puts it in his book, *An Adventure in Healing & Wholeness*, "Prayer for healing is a way to make us more receptive and willing to receive what God has already prepared for us in Christ and through the Holy Spirit."

When we pray for our own healing or the healing of another, we are not (or certainly should not be) in a begging posture. When we pray for healing, we are opening ourselves to divine intervention. We are welcoming God, inviting God to do whatever is necessary for the healing of body, mind, and spirit.

It is one thing to pray. It is quite another to pray sincerely, believing that prayer makes a difference. When you or I open our hearts to God, sharing our feelings of gratitude and sincerely thanking God, something happens inside us chemically as well as emotionally.

A psychology teacher once said most psychologists agree that a person's thoughts affect the body. "We know," said Barbara Von Frogge, "that the brain releases chemicals. More than two hundred of these [chemicals] are mood altering. So what you think, you produce in your brain chemically."

If we keep a positive mental attitude, believing that God wants us to be a whole person in every way, we enhance the probability of becoming a whole person—a happy, healthy person. We release mood-altering chemicals in our brains. A sense of well-being becomes a reality for us. Some call this kind of prayer imaging prayer.

Wagner tells this story: Matthew H. Gates was facing open-heart surgery. The surgeon came into his room, shared with Gates all the positive things about his situation. He was in the prime group for successful bypass surgery, etc. Then, the surgeon ran through a list of negative possibilities, the things that could go wrong, but were not likely to. The surgeon asked the patient, "How do you feel about all this?"

The patient, Matthew Gates, then shared an amazing story with his doctor. He told of the exercises in spiritual imaging he had been doing. He pointed to the three or four IV bags hanging above him and said, "I know that, drop by drop, they are preparing my body." Then he told the doctor, "I have two other IV's—invisible IV's, that are ministering to me. One of those invisible IV's comes from within me, the other from outside of me.

"The [Spiritual] IV that comes from outside is the result of communication with friends, family, and colleagues. Coming back to me from north, south, east, and west, from my family, my friends, my former colleagues in ministry are their prayers. Those prayers are being gathered at the feet of God, and, drop by drop by drop, they are feeding into my psyche and my soul, bringing new strength and confidence."

"The other IV comes from within myself. It is made up of all the verses, bits of scripture, hymns, lines from great prayers of the church running through my mind. When I can't remember words, I just hum the tune. Drop by drop by drop, this IV begins shaping and strengthening my outlook, my faith, my hope as I focus on the goodness, the love, the caring, the constancy of God."

The drops from this internal, spiritual IV made Matthew Gates grateful for all that had been and made him hopeful for all that was to be.

The surgeon sat quietly, listening intensely as his patient talked about these two Spiritual IV's, then there was a moment of silence. The doctor thanked Matthew Gates for sharing with him. The doctor, a devout mass-attending, Roman Catholic, shared his own faith, stating his belief that the attitude of his patients was an integral part of successful surgery.

Then the doctor produced a paper for the patient to sign authorizing the surgery. He did the neatest thing. He picked up the patient's Bible from the table beside the bed and said, "We'll make a covenant on your Bible. I offer my best surgical skills, you bring your sense of holy calm, a result of your spiritual IV's, and we will both trust God to make this a successful surgery."

With that, the surgeon left to get ready for a genuine spiritual event. Matthew Gates said, "In forty-four years in ministry, never had I experienced such a powerful moment of bonding between doctor and patient. It was truly a holy moment."

Prayer is a dynamic force that can work miracles in our lives, too. Whatever you may be facing—an illness, a chronic pain, a strained or broken relationship, a future that is uncertain or even threatening—God can help you. God can heal you physically, mentally, emotionally, spiritually, or socially.

If you will think about your particular situation, examine it as best you can in your mind. Look at it from every angle; even write it out on paper or in your journal. Then sit quietly in God's presence. Think of your loved ones and your friends who are praying for you and with you. Image them; see their faces in your mind. Try to see them praying for you. Drop by drop, this spiritual IV will bring you hope, confidence, and new strength.

Then call to mind any scriptures that can bring hope to you:

- Psalm 27:1—"The Lord is my light and my salvation; whom shall I fear" (NRSV).
- Psalm 27:14—"Be strong, and let your heart take courage, wait for the Lord" (NRSV).
- Psalm 66: 19-20—"Truly God has listened, he has given heed to the words of my prayer. Blessed be God because he has not rejected my prayer or removed his steadfast love from me" (NRSV).
- Psalm 103:17—"The steadfast love of the Lord is from everlasting to everlasting on those who trust Him" (NRSV).
- II Corinthians 4:16—"We do not lose heart...our inner nature is being renewed day by day" (NRSV).

- Romans 8:31—"If God is for us who is against us" (NRSV).
- Romans 8:39— "Nothing will be able to separate us from the love of God in Christ Jesus our Lord" (NRSV).
- John 14:27—"My peace I give you...do not let your hearts be troubled, and do not let them be afraid" (NRSV).

Recall to your mind the words of some of the songs that have meant a great deal to you through the years. Let them roll over inside you. *"I need You every hour, stay Thou near by"..."I am weak, but Thou art strong, let me walk close to Thee"..."It's me, it's me, O Lord, standin' in the need of prayer"..."Come by here Lord—Kum ba Yah"..."Why should I be discouraged"..."His eye is on the sparrow, I know He watches me"..."Breathe on me breath of God, fill me with life anew"..."Be still my soul, God is on your side"..."Nearer my God to Thee"..."Blessed assurance, Jesus is mine"..."He touched me, and made me whole"..."I've got peace like a river"..."Through many dangers, toils and snares, I have already come"..."Jesus loves me this I know"..."It is well with my soul"..."'Tis grace hath brought me safe thus far, and grace will lead me home."*

Whatever hymns or gospel songs, old or new—let their words and their tunes become, drop by drop by drop, a Spiritual IV for you as you face whatever concerns you most: an illness, a deep grief or loss, a chronic pain, a broken relationship, a difficult future, a sense of guilt. Whatever it may be, let these two Spiritual IV's help you heal.

Then, one by one, imagine the countenances of your family members, your loved ones, and your friends who pray for you. Allow their positive, warm, caring thoughts and prayers to flood over you to help you heal, to help you become a whole person. One by one, recall bits and pieces of scriptures, of old favorite songs. Let them become drops of healing, drop by drop, from a word or a tune helping you to get well.

Prayer is the primary channel through which we receive God's healing love. Let us not forget this, and let us use Spiritual IV's to help us and others.

Prayer

Blessed Jesus,

We bring unto Thy loving care and protection, on the stretchers of our prayers, all those who are sick in mind or body or soul.

Take from them, and from us, all fears, and help us to put our trust in you. Help us to feel your everlasting arms holding us close to you. Cleanse us of all resentments, jealousy, self-pity, pride, or anything else that could block your healing presence and power.

Fill us, o God, with the sense of your healing love. Touch us with your divine, transforming power that we may be healed and live our lives in such a way that we will bring glory to you.

Amen

An Exercise in Faith
Luke 18:35-43

Consider Luke 18:34-43 as it might be translated:

> As they approached Jericho, a blind man was sitting beside the road, begging from travelers. When he heard the noise of a crowd going past, he asked, "What's going on?" Someone answered, "Jesus from Nazareth is going by."
>
> The blind man began shouting, "Jesus, Son of David, have mercy on me."
>
> The crowds with Jesus tried to hush the man, but he only shouted louder, "Son of David, have mercy on me!"
>
> Jesus stopped. "Bring that man over here to me." They did. Then Jesus asked the blind man, "What do you want?"
>
> "Lord," he pleaded, "I want to see."
>
> Jesus said, "All right, begin seeing! Your faith has healed you."
>
> Instantly the man could see, and he followed Jesus, praising God. And all who saw what happened praised God too!"

In this scripture that I have paraphrased, we witness a miracle. A man, physically blind is made to see! Although you and I can see physically, we may be in the dark about some things in our own lives.

If we are honest about it, there probably are some things in our lives that we are in the dark on and not completely happy about. But we don't take time to examine them. Why?

I would like for us to sit quietly for a few moments and inquire of ourselves, what is it I am most unhappy about? Or what is it at this time that keeps me from enjoying life to its fullest?

On a 4 X 6 note card, write down a few key words or names that will call to your mind a blind spot, something you are in the dark about most of the time. What is it that creates stress in your life? What is giving you the most difficulty? Is it an attitude you have? Is it some negative habit you have developed? Stop reading for a few minutes and answer for yourself just what it you would like for Jesus to help you with.

I will confess that this in an exercise I developed many years ago and used with groups at church camp, Bethany Hills, and retreats with Senior Highs and adults. Let me share with you a few of the concerns revealed back then.

A senior high girl shared this: "My blind spot is insecurity. My happiness and wellbeing seems to depend almost entirely on what others think about me. When I don't receive affirmation from others, I find I am sad and moody. When others don't build me up, I find myself mildly depressed. I don't feel good about myself. In turn, it seems, I find fault with others. Instead of facing up to my own insecurity and asking Jesus to help me, I try to make others feel inferior."

A thirty-year-old man shared this: "My blind spot is pride and arrogance. It seems I have never been able to say, I was wrong, or I made a mistake, or please forgive me. I have trouble even thinking these thoughts. I always have to prove my point, even when I know inside that I am wrong."

A thirty-six-year-old man shared: "My blind spot is a combination of competitiveness and a win-at-all-costs attitude. From earliest childhood, I can remember a driving compulsion to win. Always, I had to be number one. I had to be the best. In grade school, it led to fights at recess time. It led to real problems with discipline and authority figures, in later years. It continued in my marriage relationship. I play one-upmanship with my spouse. I can never really give her first place."

As a spiritual director, spiritual friend, I have heard similar stories many times. Now, I don't know what your story is. I don't have any idea what your blind spot may be. I don't care to know yours and you probably don't care to know mine. But if, as followers of Christ, we desire to become whole persons, we will from time to time take a spiritual inventory, looking closely at ourselves and where we are on our life-long journey to become more Christ-like.

This little exercise in faith allows us to practice the examination of our consciences. No one is perfect. This includes every one of us here tonight. If we sincerely desire to grow spiritually, if we sincerely desire to become more Christ like, then we will recognize our blind spots. In fact, we will be brutally honest with ourselves about our spiritual needs. Like the blind man on the road to Jericho, we will acknowledge that we need Jesus!

It takes courage to look at ourselves. It takes courage to recognize our own faults. It takes courage to cry out, "Jesus, Son of David, have mercy on me!" Perhaps we find it easier to say, "Lord, have mercy on them, on him, on her. Change them, Lord, there's nothing wrong with me."

Let us truly thank God for times, when in silence and contemplation we find the courage to admit our needs, knowing Jesus will understand and help us. This brief story in Luke 18 serves as a model for us. It gives us, step by step, a way to experience spiritual insights.

1. We must have courage to cry out to Jesus, "Son of God, have mercy on me." I need You! There are blind spots in my life, areas I need your help with.

2. Use whatever senses you have to detect Jesus' nearness. The blind man couldn't see, but he could hear. He couldn't see, but he could smell. He heard the excited voices, the shuffling of sandals on the dusty road. In fact, the dust must have reached his nostrils. He knew something was happening.

3. Speak out and speak up for yourself. Jesus asks you and me, just like he asked this blind man, "What do you want me to do for you?" Be aware of what it is you need most from Jesus. Zero in on it. Be specific.

The three people that I alluded to could have said something like this: Lord Jesus, help me with self-esteem and self-confidence. Help me see my worth through your eyes. Help me not to depend so much on the affirmation and approval of other humans. Help me remember that You died on the cross for me. Help me not to depend so much on the opinions of others, but to rely on Your unconditional love for me. Help me to say and mean, "Your grace is sufficient for me Lord Jesus."

If pride and arrogance are keeping you from becoming the whole person God wants you to be, admit it. When Jesus asks,

"What do you want me to do for you?" simply and honestly admit your smugness, your tendency to look down on others, your playing games by waiting to see who's going to speak first. If pride and arrogance are blind spots in your life, ask God through Jesus to help you. Turn loose of those blind spots.

Help me Jesus! Help me say it and mean it. "I'm sorry, I made a mistake," or "please forgive me my friend." Help me Jesus not to think too highly of myself.

If winning at all costs is what drives you and at the same time drives a wedge between you and others, even good friends, let Jesus come into your life to shed light on it and help you to see that it's not the end of the world to place second or to be considered second best in the worldly competitions.

That's the beautiful thing about God's grace. When we call on Jesus and ask him in simple, plain, forthright language to help us, to heal us, he will! When we trust him, he enables us to experience a joy and fulfillment that is not dependent on what others say, or don't say about us. In other words, the accolades of our peers are no longer essential for our experiencing wholeness and a true sense of well-being.

If we have exercised our faith by writing on a 4 X 6 card the one thing we need most for Jesus to help us with, he will not fail us. He will enable us to see what needs to be done in our minds and hearts to become a whole person. (Your 4 X 6 card is for your eyes only.)

Let us remember the simple steps in being healed from spiritual blindness:

1. Have courage to admit we need Jesus
2. Sense His nearness, His closeness; remember he said, "I am with you always.
3. Speak out or write out in your journal or (4 X 6 card) your specific need if you haven't already done so.
4. Hear Him say, "What do you want me to do for you?"
5. Sit quietly looking at your note card believing with all your heart that Jesus is at work helping you.

Prayer

Eternal God,

God of grace and mercy, we thank you for your willingness to work with us to change whatever we need to change to become a whole person. We know that you can help us see ourselves as we are and you can give us the vision and the hope and the will power to become all that you created us to be. Thank you for that blind man on the road to Jericho. Thank you for his courage and his faith. May we learn from him.

In Jesus name,

Amen

Do You Believe In Miracles?
Matthew 17:14-21

The word miracle is used in common conversations quite often. "It's a miracle! It's a miracle!"

There are at least two definitions of a miracle that are usually accepted.

> Any event that appears to be unexplainable by the laws of nature and is therefore considered to be supernatural or an act of God

Examples include the parting of the Red Sea, Daniel in the lion's den, Jonah in the belly of the whale, Jesus raising Lazarus from the tomb after his being dead for four days

Now there is a second definition for miracle that I prefer to think about.

> A miracle is any event, natural or supernatural in which a person sees a revelation of God and that person's faith is increased as a result of it. (God is present in the event. God is definitely in the picture, here.)

Arthur Gordon, in his book *A Touch of Wonder* (pp122-125), tells us the story of a miracle that took place in Georgia many years ago. It is a true story of a little boy stricken with polio at the age of three. Back then, parents didn't recognize symptoms of that dread disease. The boy's mom and dad only knew that times were hard, coming out of the Great Depression. They knew they had a crippled little boy on their hands, so they carried him to the old New York City Hospital near where they lived. They left him. They never came back.

There in New York, a couple took the little fellow into their foster home, but weren't able to help him very much. It happened that this couple had relatives in Georgia, living on a large farm there. They sent this crippled little boy to their relatives in hopes that the warmer climate might help.

It also happened that on that large farm lived an extraordinary woman, Mama Jean. She worked for the owners of the farm. In a two-room cabin, she lived.

Her parents had been slaves, but people who knew her recognized that she possessed a spiritual force whose influence was felt everywhere. She was always the first person called when there was sickness. She made medicines from roots and herbs that seemed to cure just about anything. All the children around there felt like they belonged to her. They called her "Maum" Jean.

Some of the folks there, black and white, felt like that when Maum Jean prayed (simply talked to the Lord), God listened in a special way. Her heart reached out to all small, helpless things, so when this sick little boy showed up she took a special interest in him.

She detected the loneliness and withdrawal that filled his little heart. She studied his feeble efforts to overcome the damage done by the polio and, regardless of what the doctors might have said, she decided that something more ought to be done.

Maum Jean had never heard the word atrophy, but she knew that muscles could waste away unless they were used. Every night when her chores and duties were done, she would go to the little guy's room and kneel beside his bed and massage his legs.

Sometimes when he would cry out in pain, she would sing old songs or tell him stories. When her massage treatments were over, she would talk earnestly to the Lord, explaining that she was doing what she could, but that she needed God to help her. She asked God to show her or tell her when the time came for this little boy to try to walk.

There was a creek that flowed through the farm, and Maum Jean, who had never heard of hydrotherapy, knew there was strength in running water. She made her grandsons carry this little boy down to a sandy bank in the sun. There he would splash in the water while Maum Jean watched and prayed.

The boy grew taller, but there was little change in his legs. He still used crutches and still had to buckle on the clumsy braces. Night after night, Maum Jean continued the massaging and praying.

Then one morning when the boy was about eleven or twelve, Maum Jean said, "Honey, I got a surprise for you." She led him out to the yard and stood him up with his back braced against an oak tree. He could feel the rough bark supporting him. She took his crutches and braces from him, laid them on the grass and backed away from him about a dozen paces.

She said, "Honey, the Lord has spoken to me in a dream. He said it's time for you to walk. So, now, I want you to walk over here to me."

The boy's first reaction was fear. He knew he couldn't walk unaided. He had tried. He shrank back against the solid support of the tree. Maum Jean continued to speak, lovingly urging him to try.

They boy burst into tears. He begged. He pleaded. Her voice rose, suddenly, no longer gentle and coaxing, but full of strength and power, commanding, "You can walk boy! The Lord has spoken! Now, walk over here. Come here to me."

She knelt down and held out her arms. And somehow, compelled by something stronger than fear, the boy took his first faltering step, then another, and another, and another, until he reached Maum Jean and fell into her arms, both of them weeping big tears of joy.

Well, it was another two years before the boy could walk normally. But he never used the crutches again.

He grew up, took a job, and moved away. Finally he moved back near the farm where Maum Jean lived. He worked as editor of a weekly newspaper. He kept in touch. From time to time he sent her little gifts.

Then, the night came when one of Maum Jean's tall grandsons knocked on his door. It was late; there was frost in the air. "Maum Jean is dying," said her grandson and she wanted her "little boy" to come to her one more time.

The old cabin was unchanged with floors of cypress, windows with wooden shutters, no glass, and a roof of palm thatch. Maum Jean lay in bed surrounded by her family, her frail body covered by a patchwork quilt. A kerosene lamp cast a soft, dim light. She whispered the boy's name. Someone put a chair close to her bed. Her once-crippled little boy, now a strong young man, sat down and took Maum Jean's hand in his. For a long time, he sat there. She spoke softly to him. Her mind was clear. She hoped he had remembered what she taught him about faith, hope, and trust. Outside, the night wind stirred. A whippoorwill called. In the other room, a log fire sputtered. In the open fireplace, a small log snapped, throwing sparks. Everything was quiet.

Then Maum Jean's tired, weak voice said with surprise and joy, "Ooh it's so beautiful!" She gave a contented sigh and then she was gone, gone to be with her Lord, the source of her strength, the one who enabled her to help others, to help bring about miracles in their lives.

Here we have a true, documented story of a series of events that led to a miracle. A little boy on whom doctors and foster parents had given up hope, a little boy lonely, discouraged... But somehow God intervened through a simple, childlike woman who believed in miracles and helped others to believe.

Are you faced with a seemingly impossible situation? Perhaps an "incurable disease" or an impossible situation at work or at home? Are you willing to keep on believing, trusting in God and trusting in yourself? This true story I have shared has so many encouraging aspects or facets.

A catastrophic disease, infantile paralysis or polio, devastated our country for decades—the 30's, 40's, and 50's. Medical experts worked untiringly to discover a cause and a remedy. Parents lived in fear for their child. Poster children, fund raining, iron lungs keeping children alive, in hopes of finding a cure or a vaccine... Finally a vaccine was discovered by Jonas Salk. In 1963/64, our son Bill and our daughters, Cindy and Lynda, stood in line at Collierville High School to receive the vaccine. What relief!

Long before Jonas Salk discovered a miraculous medical remedy, Maum Jean had childlike faith and deep, deep love for all little creatures. Maum Jean was used by God to work a miracle in the life of a little polio-stricken boy. Maum Jean, a black woman, daughter of slaves and a little white boy abandoned in New York City Hospital were brought together by God's providence. For them, God was very much in the picture. A miracle resulted!

The main ingredients were:

1. God's presence and love
2. Perfect love, unconditional love from a woman with childlike faith
3. The deep trust the little boy had in that woman

"Perfect love casts out all fear (I John 4:18, NRSV).

Maum Jean had no fear when she stepped out in faith to massage this little boy's legs. If he had any fear in those beginning days or nights when Maum Jean came to his room to rub his little legs, massage them until they hurt, that fear was overcome as she sang songs and told him stories about God's love for him.

Then came the day when Maum Jean said, "Honey, I got a surprise for you...the Lord spoke to me in a dream...it's time for you to walk." I can only imagine the fear and anxiety that was his as he drew back rigidly against the oak tree.

But Maum Jean's deep faith in God and perfect love for her little boy overcame his fear. As she knelt and held out her arms, perfect love melted his fear, and he walked one step at a time. And God worked a miracle.

Many years later, that perfect love between Maum Jean and her little boy brought them together. On a frosty night they held hands as God completed another miracle. Maum Jean's spirit of love filled that log cabin room, and she floated into God's arms whispering, "It's so beautiful." Do you believe in miracles? Do miracles still happen?

Prayer

Dear loving God,

Worker of miracles, source of perfect love, we praise you for filling our hearts with hope, our minds with positive thoughts and our spirits with a deep sense of unity and oneness with you and others. You are all powerful and all loving. Your love removes all fear from our lives. Your power enables us to experience miracle after miracle as we perceive your presence in every circumstance of life.

Amen

Finding Wholeness Through Meaning & Purpose
Ecclesiastes 9:7-10a, Mark 12:28-31, Luke 12:25-27

In the Old Testament wisdom literature, we find a formula for holistic living. The writer of the book of Ecclesiastes is our spiritual guide. This man tried to find meaning and purpose by acquiring all the material things he could: houses, vineyards, gardens, parks, orchards, servants, great herds of livestock, silver, and gold. These things ultimately failed him. (Ecclesiastes 2:4-8, NRSV)

Next, he tried the opposite. He denounced all things material: wealth, power, big homes, and big cars. Like flower children in the American culture of the 1960's, he denounced a materialistic culture. This seemed to help him for a while, but it did not last.

He tried to find meaning and purpose through wisdom, turning to philosophy, logic, and reasoning. These things, too, left him disappointed. He next tried to escape all pain and suffering to find fulfillment before realizing that to do so was impossible. In a somewhat desperate act, he even turned to religion or a life of piety. Unfortunately the prevailing religion of his day was one of fearing God. Sensing that he could never buy into this kind of religion he rejected it, too.

This man was trying to find wholeness and happiness in things that would ultimately fail him. They brought him no lasting joy, no supreme meaning, or purpose.

How many people today are searching in all the wrong places for a sense of wholeness and well-being? Money, more money, toys, more toys, boats, 4 wheelers, the biggest, fastest vehicles on the market and on the road...

We desire the ability to think deeper, outwit and out fox all competitors so that you always come out on top. Like nine and ten year old boys playing King of the Hill, who can push the others down the hill and remain standing? The world we live in is filled with men, women and youth who are trying desperately to prove themselves to be the best, the most handsome, the most beautiful, the most talented, and the most intelligent.

Not greatly unlike the ancient writer of Ecclesiastes, we rush from one thing to another, hurrying, trying to find wholeness and inner peace in all the wrong things. We do not want to slow down and focus on those things that ultimately bring meaning and purpose to our lives—those things that make us whole persons in Jesus Christ.

The writer of Ecclesiastes lived a long time before Jesus came to live among us. But somehow, he found meaning and purpose in some of the things that Jesus himself would commend to us today, if we are to become happy, healthy, whole persons.

In Ecclesiastes 9:7-10a, we find the writer's discovery: "Go, eat your bread in gladness and drink your wine in joy, for your action was long ago approved by God" (NRSV).

- Let your clothes always be freshly washed and your head never lack ointment.
- Enjoy happiness with a woman you love (your wife) all the fleeting days of life that have been granted you under the sun.
- Whatever it is in your power to do, do with all your might.

Thinking on these words and digesting them led me to this conclusion in the year 1988. God was saying, "Harold, enjoy each moment of life to the fullest. Do your work to the best of your ability, and develop deep, lasting relationships."

Since that time I have tried to use these three guidelines to bring meaning, purpose, and wholeness into my life. I have not always succeeded, but when I have, I have experienced more happiness, fulfillment, and a deeper sense of well-being, in spite of all that may have been going on in the world around me.

In his book, *When All You've Ever Wanted Isn't Enough*, Harold Kushner explains what life should be about. (p 140-143)

Enjoy each moment to its fullest. When you savor each moment knowing that the moment won't last forever, you will find deeper meaning and joy. Moments can be eternal, even though they last only a brief time. If you really want to, you can close your eyes and remember things that happened for only a moment years ago—things like a warm hand shake or a hug from someone who was dear to you; the spectacular view of the Grand Canyon, the Smokey Mountains or a sunset off the Gulf Coast of Florida; the in depth conversation that made you know you were accepted and cared for. In your mind, you can reclaim these moments of eternity. Practice doing this from time to time.

Life is not about amassing great wealth or getting somewhere faster. It's not driving break-neck speeds with your cell phone glued to your ear. The abundant life that brings wholeness and health is about enjoying each moment to its fullest. It's about enjoying your food while sitting in the sun, rather than rushing through lunch and hurrying back to the office, the desk, and the computer. It's about savoring the beauty of God's creation, a sunset or sunrise, a hillside bursting forth in all the colors of God's palette, yellow, purple, red, brown, deep green.

God has all kinds of gifts for us: good food, beautiful skies, lakes, rivers, flowers, snow covered fields in winter, quiet moments of sharing with another human being. But we, in our pursuit of what we think will bring happiness, find ourselves so constantly on the go that God cannot find our minds, our hearts, and our spirits at home so that he can deliver these priceless gifts.

When we spend our lives looking for the grand solutions to the world's greatest problems, we miss out on the deep meaning found in the simple pleasures of good food, clean clothes, and fresh linens on the bed. When we get wrapped up in the things that are not working well for us, we often overlook the simple things that can still bring us joy, those things we can and should thank God for every day.

Whatever work or job or responsibility that is yours, do it to the very best of your ability. Give your best to your work. Work hard! Not because it will bring you money, promotions or recognition, but because it will bring you a deep sense of satisfaction as a competent person. Something deteriorating or destructive happens in the souls of people who stop caring about the quality of their work—the souls of people who simply go through the motions.

Any job worth doing at all is worth doing well, to the very best of our ability. A sloppy job is the sure sign of someone who is not a whole person deep down inside. There may be some jobs, some work, that can afford to be done poorly without hurting anyone else, but none of us, not one of us, can afford the internal spiritual cost of being sloppy in our work. It teaches us contempt for ourselves and our skills. Even if you're not going to win a Nobel Prize for your work, even if it is not going to make you rich, it can and will bring you deep meaning and a measure of wholeness if you take it seriously and do it to the very best of your ability. Whether it is work for pay or volunteer work, do it to the best of your ability. Deep meaning is found when we use our spiritual gifts, our physical gifts to the very best of our ability.

The writer of Ecclesiastes also found deep meaning in relationships. "Enjoy happiness with your wife, your husband, and your children. To love and be loved is essential for happiness and wholeness and health, be it with our spouse, our family or our friends. When the happiness and welfare of another human being is just as important as or more important to you than your own happiness and welfare, you can truly say that you love that person" (NRSV).

In a sense, this describes God's love for us. God sent his Son to live among us. To show us just how great his love is, Jesus left the glory of heaven, God's presence, to come to us, frail, imperfect human beings. He came to relate to us, live among us, love us, and forgive us.

Jesus related to all people with love—agape love—integrity, and compassion. He was firm and forthright with those who needed that from him. Jesus was assertive. He spoke the truth in love. Jesus was a good listener. He heard what was being said and what was not being said.

Jesus was secure enough in his relationship with God that he could always go the second and third mile to develop meaningful relationships with those who desired such relationships, even if it cost him dearly.

It is still true today. The living Christ will meet you and me at the point of our greatest need. He will love us, accept us, and enable us to become our best selves. He alone will empower us to develop deep meaningful relationships with our loved ones, friends, and even with those who may consider us their enemies.

So in conclusion, to become a whole person it will help if we begin intentionally to enjoy each moment of life to its fullest, if we undertake every task with the determination to do it well, and if we develop even deeper relationships with others.

I suggest that you sit quietly and think about those special moments that you have experienced in the past—moments of eternity that bring you joy. Thank God for them. Think about the work you are called to do, and promise yourself you will do it to the best of your ability. Finally, think about your relationship with Christ. Are you working from your side to deepen that relationship with prayer and by focusing on the teachings of Jesus?

Pray that God will enable you to find wholeness and health by living each moment to its fullest, by doing your work to the very best of your ability and by working at deeper, more meaningful relationships.

Prayer

Dear God,

Help us not to overlook the simple things that make for wholeness and health. Slow us down so that we can enjoy each moment of life. Restore in us a desire to do whatever work we are called upon to do with vigor and genuine interest. Help us to celebrate the intimate relationship you offer to us through your son, our Lord and Savior.

Amen

The Healing Power of Touch
Matthew 8:1-4, 14, 15

We could say that Jesus touched, in some way, every person he made whole, every person he healed. Some he touched with his hands. Others reached out to touch Him. With others, it was intense eye contact. Touch is essential for health: physical, mental, emotional, and spiritual.

Dr. Scott Morris of the Church Health Center wrote a column for the Commercial Appeal (Monday, June 5, 2006) "Touch is a Basic Human Need." He explained how he, as a young doctor, called on a patient who was HIV positive. It was his first such call. Just before Scott entered the patient's hospital room, he looked at his chart. The nurse had written in large letters the word AIDS on the top of the chart.

Scott sat down, asked the usual new-patient questions. But before he could broach the question of AIDS, the patient, a young man, touched Scott's knee and said, "It's okay Doc, you can't get it from just talking to me."

Scott looked down at his own hands and realized what his patient must have observed. His hands were trembling, and he also realized he was sweating.

Scott took a few deep breaths and admitted to the young man that he was the first patient with Aids that he had called on. Suddenly, their roles were reversed, the patient was teacher, and the doctor was student. The patient began to cry as he told Dr. Scott Morris that the hardest part about living with Aids. "No one ever touches me," he said.

In Dr. Morris' column, he goes on to reflect on the importance of touch:

> The absence of touch in doctor's offices is a profound problem. The most common complaint people have about their doctors is "she/he never touches me." Physicians have come to rely so much on technology and pills that the healing power of touch has become a lost art.
>
> Touching in general is something we, as a society, seem to value less and less. In our churches, we often dread "passing the peace" and many people shake hands rather

than embracing each other with a warm hug. Yet, repeated scientific studies have documented that touch truly has a healing power that is not easily explained away.

According to the Gospels, Jesus did not hesitate to use physical touch in communicating God's love. In Matthew 8:1-4, a leper came to Jesus and said, "Lord, if you choose, you can make me clean" (NRSV). Jesus stretched out his hand and touched the leper. "I choose to heal you, be made clean" (NRSV). In Matthew 8:14-15, Jesus goes to Peter's house. He finds Peter's mother-in-law lying in bed with a fever. He touches her hand, the fever leaves her and she gets up and begins to serve Jesus.

In Mark 8:22-25, some people bring a blind man to Jesus and beg Jesus to heal him, touch him. Jesus takes the man by the hand, leads him out of the village, puts saliva on his eyes and the man can see. Jesus asks the man, "Can you see anything?"

"I can see people, but they look like trees walking."

Jesus laid his hands on the man's eyes a second time, looked intently at the man and the man's sight was completely restored. He could see everything clearly (NRSV).

Touch is indeed an important part of healing. I firmly believe that Dr. Scott Morris is right in his observations and recommendations concerning touch. God created so many things that are good for us. Unfortunately, we distort much of what he created, making of it something contrary to His intentions.

Food and drink were intended to keep us healthy and fit physically. What do we do? We overindulge and ruin our health.

Shelter and transportation were intended by God to help us remain protected and mobile in order to serve Him better. What do we do? We long for a bigger home—a mansion! Only a bigger, faster car—an Escalade, Porsche, Hummer, etc.—will satisfy our ego desires.

The key to a healthy, happy life is not to have all we desire or crave. It is, instead, to desire or require only the necessities, the basics. Part of our unhealthy lifestyle is the result of feeling we must have more and more of everything.

Now, back to this thing of touching and being touched... Our culture has distorted true love and intimacy by replacing it, or trying to replace it, with racy, sensuous, lustful, physical contact.

What was once considered absolutely sinful, disgraceful, lewd, and sexually taboo is now bombarded into family living rooms and dens. Much of it is looked at, laughed about, and condoned. Is it any wonder that there is so much confusion when it comes to a simple, warm touch or embrace?

Our American culture has totally distorted what God created as good, wholesome and pure. As Dr. Scott Morris said, "[Touch] is an essential ingredient to a healthy life."

Jesus took little children on his lap, hugged them, tussled their hair, laughed with them, and blessed them with genuine care and concern (Luke 10:13, NRSV).

Jesus took a deaf man aside on one occasion and put his finger in the deaf mans ears. He used saliva to moisten his fingers, touched the deaf man, looked up to Heaven, and said, "Be opened." Then, the man could hear.

On the Mt. of Transfiguration, Peter, James and John fell to the ground when a voice came from Heaven saying, "This is my beloved son with whom I am well pleased." Jesus came, touched them saying, "get up, now, do not be afraid" (Matthew 17:7, NRSV).

In Matthew 9:29, two blind men came to Jesus. He asked them "Do you believe?" They said, "yes." Jesus touched them. They could see. Their eyes were opened (NRSV).

We are here tonight because we want to be whole, healthy men, women, and children of God. We need to sing and praise God for His desire to touch us.

Touch me Jesus, touch my mind. Heal my negative thoughts. Help me to allow only pure and positive thoughts to occupy my mind. When anything ugly tries to occupy space there, help me replace it with thoughts of you and your love. Transform my thinking by the power of your presence. Cause the radiance of your love to bring light into every dark corner.

Touch me Jesus. Touch my body at the point of each and every ailment and pain: my back and my legs, my feet, my shoulders, my neck and my head. Touch me and heal me. Give me strength to endure until ultimate healing occurs.

Touch me Jesus. Touch my relationships. Remove any brokenness, any regrets, any hard feelings. Help me to truly forgive and to receive forgiveness. Make me sensitive to others and their needs, especially those closest to me. Enable me not to think too highly of myself. Help me to truly treat others as I want to be treated.

Touch me Jesus. Touch my spirit, my soul. Kindle in my heart the fire of your love; fill me with love and joy, peace and patience, kindness and generosity, gentleness and faithfulness, and self-control. May your spirit become my spirit, Lord Jesus.

Christ touched. Freely, purely, lovingly, He touched others to enhance healing and wholeness.

If Christ abides in us as He promised, then we become His hands today, in a very real way. We can enhance the lives of others as we touch them on behalf of Jesus.

James K. Wagner, in *The Healing Ministry of Christ*, rewrote St. Francis of Assisi's peace prayer for healing.

Prayer

Gracious, loving, caring God,
Source of all healing and wholeness,
Make us instruments of Your healing.
When we are weak and in pain, help us to rest;
When we are anxious, help us to wait patiently;
When we are fearful, help us to trust in You;
When we are lonely, help us to love;
When we place You apart from us
*   help us to know that You are still near.*
Healing God, grant us not so much to demand everything
*   from ourselves, as to allow others to help us;*
Grant us not so much to seek escape, as to face ourselves
*   and to learn the depths of Your love.*
For it is in being uncertain and not in control,
*   that we find true faith;*
In knowing the limits of mind and body,
*   that we find wholeness of spirit;*
In passing through death that we find life
*   that lasts forever.*
In the name of Christ Jesus, our Savior,
*   Our Healer, our Lord, we offer ourselves to You.*

Amen.

The Healing Power of Music

All great art has a healing quality, be it visual, performing, or vocal. Men and women have long been drawn to the Creator God, the ultimate source of all creativity and healing.

To sit in an art gallery and study the great masterpieces, to watch the graceful movements of ballet dancers, or to drink deeply of the haunting and healing combination of melody, harmony, rhythm, timbre, and resonance that flows from the mind and heart of a Johannes Brahms, Ludwig Von Beethoven, or Johann Christian Bach, is to put oneself in the healing flow of God's love.

I cannot tell you how blessed Dot and I have been listening to the healing music of our chancel choir. Music calms the spirit, stills the soul, and stirs the heart. One does not need a degree in music—voice, piano or otherwise—to experience healing in one's soul as a result of music itself. Even simple gospel songs bring wholeness.

Like all other forms of art, music is very subjective. What pleases one person may, in fact, turn another person off. Find time to nurture your spirit and soul with the music that comforts you, speaks to you. Keep close at hand the CD's, tapes, DVD's, or videotapes that bring comfort to you. Healing will take place.

Recently, I checked out a videotape from our library here at Lindenwood. On it are the stories behind five of our most beloved hymns. The cassette by Questar, Inc. is the inspiration for this homily. It is entitled *Amazing Grace: 5 Hymns that Changed the World.*

Three of these hymns were given birth by someone who, at that time, was going through tragedy or pain, or working through brokenness in his life. The other two were given birth by persons in praise and thanksgiving to our Creator God.

When we look beyond the lyrics and melodies into the lives of these men, we discover the healing quality of music, as it was being composed even before it was sung or performed. Music emanating from one's soul brings a measure of healing and wholeness. These truly great hymns speak to us today. We experience as much today as those who first heard these songs years ago. God can speak to us through hymns and treasured anthems. Music is a precious gift from the heart of God to the soul of man.

Great hymns personalize our relationship with God. Music is a powerful vehicle that opens our hearts to the things of God. Great hymns become familiar friends, bringing a legacy of faith and strength. Great hymns, when sung by simple followers of Christ, can become defining moments of deep encounter between God and humanity. They can enhance our becoming whole persons.

Shortly after the Civil War, Chicago became the center of a booming commerce. The shores of Lake Michigan became the nerve center of businesses where men of vision became extremely wealthy.

A certain man with great knowledge in law and real estate went to Chicago from New York. In a short time, he was one of the wealthiest persons in the Midwest. He knew what to invest in and what to avoid. He was wise, and in his wisdom, he recognized that financial wealth was only a part of his blessings. He was looked on by his peers as a man of integrity. He had their admiration.

His wife, Anna, and his small children were the family he adored. He was very active in his church. He supported the evangelist, Dwight L. Moody. These two things brought him tremendous spiritual fulfillment. He was overwhelmed at his blessings.

Then, in 1871, his life, so rich with joy, became devastated by a series of tragedies. He and Anna's only son died of scarlet fever that winter. And then while they were still grieving that loss, disaster struck all of Chicago. In a raging fire, completely out of control, cost 300 people their lives in the downtown area. Within 24 hours, many of this man's extensive real estate investments went up in flames. Yet, he set about helping others who had lost even more than himself.

In the Fall of 1873, his spiritual mentor, Dwight L. Moody traveled to England to spread the gospel there. Feeling a change of scenery would be good for his own family, he purchased six fares, for himself, Anna and their four young daughters. However, a day before departure time for the luxury passenger ship, this man received word that it was absolutely essential for him to remain in Chicago for an important business meeting concerning his extensive losses in the fire. He insisted that his wife and girls go on without him and promised he would join them as soon as possible.

November 11, 1873 the ship departed. Four days into the voyage, the ship encountered dense fog in the North Atlantic. As a result of the dense fog, a steel hulled English sailing ship rammed the luxury liner broad side. It sank in less than twelve minutes. Two hundred twenty-six passengers perished, including the man's four daughters.

An hour after the tragedy, Anna, the man's beloved wife, was pulled from the icy waters. When she finally reached safety in Wales, she sent a cable to her husband with two words on it. The cable read, "Saved alone," meaning that she alone was saved while the remainder of their beloved family was lost in the deep, dark, icy waters of the North Atlantic Ocean.

First the loss of his infant son, then the devastating fire in Chicago, great financial loss and now, his four beloved daughters were gone! In unimaginable pain, he clung to his faith in God. He confided to a close friend, "I am trusting the Lord, thank God, in spite of my great loss."

He immediately booked passage for himself to England to join his wife in her bereavement. The journey was long. He spent hours deep in prayer and contemplation. Less than a week into his voyage the captain said to him, "I believe we are passing over the spot where the luxury liner went down with your family aboard.

As this grieving father looked down into the watery grave of his four girls, a torrent of emotion rushed from his broken heart. He identified with Job in the Old Testament. He said later, he had gone through some real deep times, but never anything like this.

"Through it all," he said, "as it got darker and darker, somehow the light of Christ and God's promises began to shine brighter in my heart. I found I couldn't do anything but express myself in a way that I had a gift for. I was not a poet by trade, but I love to write poetry. Without a moment's hesitation the testimony began to flow from my heart through my pen."

In that extraordinary moment, sorrow became hope. He was strengthened by the assurance that he would, some day be reunited with his children. In his cabin, he wrote one of the most profound expressions of faith ever recorded. Horatio Spafford was his name. You will find his immortal words on page 561 in your chalice

Hymn Book. Written, as we have indicated in 1873 by Horatio G. Spafford, set to music in 1876 by Philip P. Bliss, this hymn has brought to many broken hearts deep healing and a measure of wholeness and hope.

> *When peace like a river*
> *Attendeth my way,*
> *When sorrows like sea billows roll,*
> *Whatever my lot, Thou has taught me to say,*
> *It is well, it is well with my soul.*
>
> *It is well, (it is well),*
> *With my soul (with my soul),*
> *It is well, it is well with my soul.*
>
> *Though Satan should buffet,*
> *Though trials should come,*
> *Let this blest assurance control,*
> *That Christ has regarded my helpless estate,*
> *And hath shed his own blood for my soul.*
>
> *It is well, (it is well),*
> *With my soul (with my soul),*
> *It is well, it is well with my soul.*

It is marvelous the way he wrote it. We feel that we are out on the sea with him. We are all out on the sea of life and regardless of what happens to us, whether it be physical, financial, or whatever, God will never leave us. He will not forsake us. We can say, "my body may cry out, but it is well with my soul."

If it is truly well with our soul we are becoming whole persons. There is healing power in music. Especially in this beloved hymn, to know we are accepted and loved by God.

Some songs are written in a moment of inspiration. Like "It Is Well with My Soul," others take much longer, like, "How Great Thou Art." This classic hymn of hope and healing was written over a period of many years, decades in fact. It was in actually penned by two authors, not one—a young pastor in Sweden and a devout missionary from Great Britain.

In the summer of 1885, Carl Boberg, a young Swedish pastor, was strolling though the countryside. A thunderstorm broke across the hill. He took refuge in an abandoned farmhouse and watched in amazement as the display of God's awesome power revealed itself. This spectacular unleashing of God's tremendous power, driving rain, lightning, and thunder, followed by the clearing of the sky, a rainbow, and the song of a thrush, plus the church bells sounding in the distance—this experience caused him to fall to his knees in humble adoration and praise the god who created it all and held it all in His hands.

That evening he wrote a poem, "O Great God," depicting what he had seen. He read it to his congregation. It was published in a local periodical, and then the words were sung to a traditional Swedish folk melody.

In 1907, Carl Boberg's poem, now a hymn, was translated into German. Then, 20 years later, a Russian version was published. However, it wasn't until Stuart Hine, a British missionary, heard it sung in a small Ukrainian church that a remarkable chain of events occurred, propelling this song into world wide popularity.

Hine was captivated by the song because of the natural beauty that surrounded him. The beautiful, natural surroundings through which he hiked stimulated a deep appreciation for God's creation. He observed many young Swedish students there hiking and singing this song as the walked along.

Its tune and words seemed to carry to heaven what was on their hearts. Hine was so moved that he set to English the words of this hymn of praise. Because he was so thrilled and inspired by God's grandeur and power the first stanzas in English, came easily to him.

O Lord my God! When I in awesome wonder
Consider all the worlds thy hands have made
I see the stars, I hear the rolling thunder,
Thy power throughout the universe displayed.

Then sings my soul, my Savior God to thee;
How great thou art, how great thou art!
Then sings my soul, my Savior God to thee;
How great thou art, how great thou art!

When through the woods and forest glades I wander,
And hear the birds sing sweetly in the trees;
When I look down from lofty mountain grandeur
And hear the brook and feel the gentle breeze;

Then sings my soul, my Savior God to thee;
How great thou art, how great thou art!
Then sings my soul, my Savior God to thee;
How great thou art, how great thou art!

During the next few years, the hymn stayed alive in Hines imagination as he ministered and distributed Bibles. In the Ukraine, he became aware that many dear souls had not had the privilege of reading for themselves the story of God's great sacrifice through his son, a gift that far surpassed anything he had given us through nature and creation.

An elderly woman read aloud the story of Christ's crucifixion. As she did her friends fell to their knees crying out to God in thanksgiving for His great sacrifice and love for them. Many of them realized for the very first time the true magnitude of God's love for them as individuals. "God loves *me* this much!"

Inspired by this event, the third stanza came to Hine:

And when I think that God, his Son not sparing,
Sent him to die, I scarce can take it in;
That on the cross, my burden gladly bearing,
He bled and died to take away my sin;

Hine continued to think about this hymn that had possessed so much of his mind and heart. With three stanzas written in English verse, he had no idea it would be another decade before it would be revealed to him the words for a fourth or final stanza.

1939 saw the beginning to WWII in Europe. The horrors and devastation caused Hine and other missionaries to be forced to leave Russia. He returned to England. There he ministered to his homeland in its bombed out condition. War refugees from Europe, some 250,000, were in England seeking temporary asylum. One evening while speaking to a group of those war refugees, it was asked of them "Do you have any questions?"

One young woman echoed the thoughts of nearly all of them. "When are we going home? When can we go home?"

Hine found in that woman's question the inspiration for the fourth and final stanza.

> *When Christ shall come with shout of acclamation*
> *And take me home, what joy shall fill my heart.*
> *Then I shall bow in humble adoration,*
> *And there proclaim, my God, how great thou art!*

After these many years Hine's work in English was completed. The door was opened for the immortal power and beauty of this song to spread throughout the world. At the Billy Graham crusade in Madison Square Garden in 1957, George Beverly Shea sang it on opening night. Cliff Barrows said that during the 100 services held in that 1957 crusade this song was sung 99 times!

Within another decade it was translated into dozens of languages and sang in every corner of the earth. In one century, 1885-1985, this song became one of the most beloved of all hymns ever written and sung.

I once mentioned to you on another occasion how this song impacted my own decision for ministry. I have come more and more to experience healing and wholeness through it as well.

God gives each one of us a gift of creativity, I sincerely believe this. When you are hurting or when you feel extremely blessed, write your thoughts and feelings down, hold on to them, reflect on them, for they are a precious gift of God to your soul.

Prayer

Eternal, loving, Creator we praise you tonight for the blessed gift of music, melodies, lyrics, harmony, rhythm and resonance. How they touch our souls through our senses. We thank your composers, writers, musicians who bring healing into our lives. We claim the healing power of music for ourselves here and now.

Amen.

Jesus is My Best Friend
John 15:12-15

My hunch is this. I give you a list of names. That list will have no meaning to you at all. Perhaps my wife Dot will make sense of the list because she has known most of them: Junior Porter, Gene Curtis, Jack Tennison, Buddy Barton, Randy Payne, Earl Cunningham.

At some point in my life from childhood to adulthood I considered each one to be my best friend. It was at these times that they were important in my life:

- Playing street games, hide and seek, etc., or sitting on front steps or a sidewalk curb telling ghost stories or teasing girls: age 9-10.
- Attending Sunday School, misbehaving, teasing or aggravating girls: age 12-13.
- Learning the skills, passing Boy Scout requirements for an advancement: age 13-16.
- Going places as two couples or shooting pool while the girls played bunco: age 20's-30's.
- Living as next-door neighbors, working together painting Coca-cola signs: age 30's-40's.
- Working together as leaders in the church, praying together, planning together, traveling with our wives, enjoying many family events together, Christmas, Thanksgiving, birthdays, etc.: age 40's-70's.

In each case, I felt some need for deep friendship being met. Hopefully it was a mutual relationship. Andrew Jackson it was, I believe, who said, "To have a friend, you must be a friend."

I read about a young newspaper reporter who years ago in a large Midwest city recognized an automobile magnate. "Mr. Ford, I admire you very much. Could I have the privilege of shaking your hand?" the young man said, impulsively.

Henry Ford extended his hand and just out of the blue (we would say) asked the young reporter, "Who is your best friend?"

Surprised by the question, the young man stammered at a loss of words. Ford took a piece of paper from his pocket, wrote on it, and handed it to the young man. The paper said, "Your best friend is he who brings out the very best in you," and was signed by Henry Ford.

The young man carried that scrap of paper with him for years, finally lost it, but never forgot the message. For that young man, only one person could fulfill the role of his best friend: Jesus Christ, the Carpenter from Nazareth. That young man went on to become an outstanding minister, writer, lecturer, who had tremendous influence on the lives of hundreds of thousands of people. His writings still inspire people to become their best selves.

Dot and I spent several different weeks with that man: Norman Vincent Peale. Dot asked his wife Ruth, "Out of all the books that Dr. Peale has written do you have a favorite?"

"As a matter of fact I do. This book," she said, holding up *The Positive Power of Jesus Christ*.

Since that time, late 1980's or early 1990's, it has become one of our favorites. You can pick it up, start with any chapter, and become inspired by the way Christ has touched and transformed the lives of so many people.

Over and over, men and women in all stations of life have found the one person who can bring out the very best in them to be Jesus the Christ.

There is no limit to the blessings you and I will receive when Jesus is our best friend. One beautiful thing about his friendship is this: We do not outgrow it. Unlike Junior Porter and the other boyhood friends, Jesus' friendship is forever. It is unlike Randy and Earl, whose friendship was in some sense limited to their physical presence, (both have gone on the be with God.) Nevertheless, their memories and their influence lingers.

The friendship offered by the living Christ is never ending and never changing. He is with us 24/7, day and night.

He is the one friend you and I need, for as I have said, there is no limit to the blessings you and I will experience as we receive Him as our dearest friend.

- First, we will receive the fullness of His love.
- Second, his close friendship will keep us from becoming a lesser person than we were created to be.

74

- Third, being friends with Jesus will empower us to overcome life's deepest problems, deepest hurts, including health problems.

In summary then, if Jesus is your best friend, you will experience abundant life, a wholeness you can never experience without Him.

The first step in becoming a friend with anyone is getting to know that person and allowing that person to know you. Look at Jesus. In five chapters of John's Gospel, he reveals much about himself.

- Jesus is light and life. He gives those who believe in him, a reason for living. (Chapter 1)
- He turns water into wine, saving the wedding hosts from being embarrassed and filled with shame. He is concerned about ordinary people in everyday events. (Chapter 2)
- He meets in secrecy with a sincere Pharisee who is searching for new life, longing to experience the Spirit of God anew and afresh. (Chapter 3)
- He meets with an outcast Samaritan woman at a well, engages her in conversation, helps her face up to what she is doing to destroy herself. He gives her living water and newfound hope. (Chapter 4)
- He confronts in love an invalid man by a pool. (For 38 years this poor soul had been helpless.) In love and compassion, Jesus tells him, "Arise, pick up your mat and walk. You are healed!"

In these five chapters of John's Gospel, we witness the power of His presence. We see His genuine caring and love for all kinds of people in all kinds of situations.

So in these five chapters we see firsthand (1) the fullness of His love (2) His power enabling people to fulfill their potential, keeping them from becoming and remaining less than God created them to be (3) His power restoring them to health and helping them overcome their deepest problems.

Let's look at these three:

1. Claim His love for yourself.

He loves you, truly loves you as no other would or could love you. Your spouse loves you. Your children love you. You may have a close friend who loves you. But remember this: No one, no other human being will ever love you like Jesus loves you. His reason for coming to live among us was to make us aware of just how greatly God loves us. This is no small or insignificant matter. For us to be aware that we are loved deeply and completely by the wisest, most exciting, most loving and caring person who ever walked this Earth, the most incredible and amazing personality who ever walked among us—this is something to truly celebrate! We are loved with unlimited love! The person with the greatest love and passion for life itself is the one I want for my best friend. No one loves me more than Jesus. I want Him to be my best friend because his love and total acceptance of me brings out the very best that is within me.

Dot is second only to Christ. But she is second. She knows that, and is happy with it that way, would have it no other way. The same is true with me. I know I am her second love; Jesus is her first love.

Sometimes when I am aware that she is in prayer, I am also aware that she is communicating with her best friend, thanking Him or interceding on behalf of her children, or grandchildren. Jesus is her best friend. He loves her even more deeply than I do, and that's going some. His love can do far more for her than my love. I recognize that truth.

2: When Jesus is my best friend, I become a better person.

He encourages me, believes in me, and reminds me that I am a child of God. He will not let me become a mean, vindictive, prejudiced person if I stay close to Him!

A year or two ago I talked by phone with a young man whose father had just died. He had attended the funeral. There were a total of fourteen people present. This young man's father had been a brilliant person. He earned his PhD, had been a key lay leader in his church at one time, an elder, and served his country as a fighting marine during the Korean conflict. His wife stood by him, encouraged him.

But then something went wrong. Pride took over. He evidently felt he no longer needed Jesus as his friend. He lost his way. Jesus and his teaching were no longer important to this man. He left his wife and two children, turned his back on the church, became a different person. The son said to me, "Dad tried in his last days to reconcile with others, but it just wasn't in him to do so." Then with great emotion he spoke these words to me over the phone. "My dad died a mean, nasty, ugly old man. It was so sad. He did try to compliment me on what I've been able to do with my life. He even acknowledged that mom had done a good job raising me and my sister."

The sad truth about this man's life is that he had alienated himself from those who could have brought out the best in him, especially Jesus Christ.

Without Jesus as our best friend we, too, may drift into becoming something less than God created us to be. The next time you are tempted to do something mean or ugly to someone else, even if you feel they deserve it—the next time bitterness begins to enter your heart, remember Jesus is with you. He will help you rise above smallness, littleness, meanness, ugliness. He will keep you from becoming a mean, nasty, old person. This leads us to the third reason to have Jesus as our best friend.

3: He gives us the power to persevere.

He will enable us to overcome any tragedy, any difficulty, any problem facing us.

I don't know what you may be facing: Lack of self-esteem? Financial problems? A life-threatening bad habit? Jesus as your best friend will give you the strength and the guidance to rise above any of these.

Just remember this:

- If He can bring new life and hope into lives of tax collectors, if He can take a group of unlearned fishermen and change the course of history, He can give you the power to do something good, fine, and positive with your life.

- If He can turn water into wine, He can take your humdrum, dreary days, add sparkle to them, and give you cause to rejoice and celebrate.
- He was willing to meet Nicodemus, the Pharisee at night and lead him, step by step, to a deep awareness of his need to be born again. He will do the same for us if we are humble enough to ask and to follow Him.
- If Jesus lovingly helped that poor woman at the well to face up to her self-destructive ways and gave to her hope and a measure of self-respect, don't you believe He loves you and will help you regain a measure of self-respect? Absolutely, most assuredly! If Jesus had the power and the will and desire to heal a man crippled for thirty-eight years, do you not believe he can heal you of anything that limits you mentally, spiritually or physically. He can make you whole and send you on your way. If you will let Jesus call you his friend, if you will do your best to obey his commands by loving him, loving yourself, and loving others, you will never, ever become anything less than He created you to be. And you will have his power to live a victorious life here and now!

Prayer

Loving God,

We come to you tonight claiming your Son as our best friend. In doing so, we open ourselves to you to receive blessing upon blessing. We praise you that you call us your friend. We praise you that you do not look upon us as servants. (Servants don't know what their master is doing.) You have made crystal clear to us what you are doing, healing, curing, loving, encouraging and never leaving us. Praise you oh Holy Father.

In Christ's Name,

Amen

The Healing Power of the Sacraments
I Corinthians 11:23-26

As we began our third year offering this unique worship service, we did so emphasizing the importance of the sacraments in our becoming a whole person in Christ.

Every time we were led in worship I have said something like this: "It is here at the table that we experience the healing power of Christ more than at any other time or place. We bring our insufficiencies to the all-sufficient Christ, and we receive His presence in a profound way, His healing presence."

Sacraments are sacred moments that involve our physical senses: touch, sight, and sound. As we step into the waters of Baptism we feel the water against our skin. We hear the ripples as the water flows over us. We see the lights reflected off the water, either sunlight, moonlight, or the ceiling lights of the sanctuary. So Baptism is also an important sacrament representing new birth, a new start, a cleansing—not physical but spiritual, mental, and emotional. We are buried with Christ, and we are raised from the Baptismal waters with new hope.

Now, under normal conditions, we experience Baptism only once. But we have the opportunity to relive our Baptism every time we witness the Baptism of another person. It is a time to remember that Christ died, was buried, and rose again physically. It is a time to remember that we, too, have died to an old way of life that was self-centered, and we have risen from Baptismal waters to live forever with Christ. We take on a new identity. We are one with Christ as we become a part of the Body of Christ, the Church. This in itself should enhance our wholeness, our oneness with Christ and with others. The sacrament of Baptism is an important part of our becoming a whole person.

Then there is the sacrament of Holy Communion. We know well the importance, the value, of this sacred act of remembrance. The Eucharist, the Lord's Supper, is one of Christ's healing gifts to His church. Let us think of Holy Communion as sacramental therapy, a channel of God's grace, communicating health, wholeness, and salvation. When I use the word therapy, I mean any helpful method or treatment that brings about healing and wholeness.

There are certain elements of worship that more readily enhance and facilitate the healing process. The sacrament of Holy Communion is the primary source of healing. When we participate in Holy Communion, the reenacting of that experience in the upper room, we come in direct contact with the source of life, health, and salvation.

Paul was on target when he wrote to the church at Corinth (I Corinthians 11:23-26). Notice how he purposely ties together the Lord's Supper with the life, death, resurrection, and the coming again of Christ. It is all there, the Gospel complete! Every time we are truly focused at the table we recognize that the total Gospel message is here. It is rooted in the atonement made possible by Christ. It is a bit ironic that the worst day of His life, the day he was horribly put to death, we know as Good Friday. To be at one with God in Christ is to be healed at the deepest, most significant level. In our daily journey toward wholeness of body, mind, spirit, and relationships, we need the Grace of God as experienced in this sacrament of Holy Communion.

Quite frequently someone will ask, "How often should a Christian participate in Holy Communion?" The answer to this question is found in another question: "How often do we need to experience the love, the mercy, the forgiveness, the grace of God in our lives?"

We cannot overstate the health enhancing possibilities of the sacrament of Holy Communion; it will enhance our health if we develop a keener understanding and appreciation of adoration, praise, and thanksgiving. If we understand the importance of confession, forgiveness, and the assurance of pardon that emanate from the act of Holy Communion we enhance our becoming a whole person in Christ.

There is a traditional prayer that has been prayed by Christians as they come to the table. It goes something like this:

We do not presume to come to this, your table, o merciful Lord, trusting in our own righteousness, but in your great mercy. We are not worthy so much as to pick up the crumbs of bread from under this table. But you, O God have love and mercy for us, as unworthy as we are. Allow us therefore, gracious Lord, to partake of this sacrament of your son Jesus

Christ, so that we may walk in newness of life, healed and restored to His likeness. Help us to dwell in Him and Him to dwell in us, we pray.

When we focus on Christ who is the host at the table, we drink deeply of His healing love. We experience the abundant, holistic life He promised his followers. Those who preside at the table, clergy and laity, are secondary in this sacred drama. We come here to be with Christ, fully aware of his risen presence as we commune with Him in spirit.

To come in deep faith to participate in the breaking of bread and in the drinking of the cup is to participate in the very life, spirit, and presence of Christ. To become one with Christ always enhances and promotes health and wholeness.

Many Christians have given witness to the strong relationship between Holy Communion and healing. Martin Luther called the Eucharist "the medicine of God." A devout Christian registered nurse said, "The Eucharist for me is a spiritual booster shot, an immunization against disease and evil." Another spiritual giant, Charles De Foucauld, said something like this, "Never miss a Holy Communion through your own fault; Communion is more than life, more than all the wealth of the world, more than the whole universe, Communion is Jesus. How can you prefer anything else to Jesus?"

Much of what I am sharing with you here is taken from *An Adventure in Healing and Wholeness*, chapter six, by James K. Wagner. It was our blessing, Dot's and mine, to spend five days with Dr. Wagner at Lake Junaluska several years ago.

I have personally experienced moments of healing and wholeness while partaking of Holy Communion on many occasions. In 1970, at the World Convention in Adelaide, Australia, I felt a sense of oneness with Christians from around the globe as Dot and I participated in Holy Communion with hundreds of followers of Christ, speaking several languages. In 1980, again at the World Convention, in Honolulu, Hawaii, we broke bread and sipped the cup in worship. We felt a deep sense of wholeness with Christians from every major continent. In 1988, in Aukland, New Zealand, in 1992 at Long Beach, California, and again in Calgary,

Canada we experienced the healing presence of Christ as we shared in Holy Communion.

As a result of these World Conventions, we have a collection of small communion cups in our home. We treasure them. Just last week, Dot and I partook of Holy Communion in our bedroom at home as our congregation celebrated the Lord's Supper. We listened to the worship service by radio. We sipped the juice from cups received at Long Beach in 1992.

We need the healing power of Christ in our lives. Dot and I felt the need for healing as we had missed church two Sundays due to an accident and illness. Praise God, He never fails us in our deepest needs. God heals us.

All of these things point out the importance of Holy Communion in our lives. Our Elders carry Holy Communion into homes and hospitals on a regular basis.

Another important scripture, in addition to I Corinthians 11:23-26, is Luke 24:13-35. In this passage, we find mercy, compassion, patience, wisdom, and power flowing from Christ Jesus into the lives of Cleophas and his companion as they walk home to Emmaus. In this passage of scripture, we find that Jesus, unrecognized, enquired of them, "What are you two talking about?" He opens the door for them to share their broken heartedness. Their response was, "Haven't you heard about the horrible turn of events that has taken place in Jerusalem? Jesus of Nazareth, mighty in deed and word, we had hoped that He was the one to redeem Israel, to set us free. But He was arrested, condemned to death, and crucified. We were told by some of the women of our group that when they went to his tomb this morning, his body was not there. They said that angels told them Jesus is alive. Some of our group then went to the tomb, but they didn't see Him. We're totally confused" (NRSV).

Jesus, with compassion, patience, and power, reminds these two that it is all a fulfillment of the scriptures. Beginning with Moses He interprets to them all the things in scripture about himself.

By now, walking and talking, they come near their village. Jesus walks ahead of them as if He is going on. "Stay with us," they plead. "The day is almost over" (NRSV).

He goes into their home. They sit down to eat. Jesus takes the bread, blesses it and breaks it and serves them. A light goes on in their minds. It all makes sense! Their eyes were opened. They recognized Him. He vanishes from their sight. They look at each other. "Were not our hearts burning within us on the road as He opened the scriptures and explained things to us" (NRSV)?

They get up and return to Jerusalem, find the eleven disciples and others, and share with them what had happened on the road, but more than that, how Jesus had been made known to them in the breaking of the bread.

Their hope is restored! All of life looks brighter because they recognized the risen Christ in the sacrament of Holy Communion.

I don't know where you are in terms of your health, physical, mental or emotional. But I know one thing for sure; Jesus can help you just as he helped the two on the road. He cleared up their confusion. He healed their broken heartedness. He gave them hope. Once they sat at the table and shared the bread they were given new life, new hope and new joy. It is the same with us. Holy Communion is the "medicine of God." It is a "spiritual booster shot. It immunizes us against evil and disease."

It is my prayer that we will experience the fullness of God's healing power every time we sip the cup and eat the bread.

Prayer

Bless us, dear God, with a full, deep, lasting awareness of just how much you desire for us to experience good health every time we partake of Holy Communion.
In Christ's Holy Name

Amen

The Healing Power of Helping Others
Mark 2:1-6

Does focusing on the needs of others—getting outside of ourselves—in fact, bring about healing? As I have observed the actions and interests of men and women who are involved in simple acts of kindness for others, it has become my opinion that these kind helpers seem to be free of minor irritations that consume the self-centered persons who constantly whine about their bad luck, their misfortunes.

In no way am I saying that those people who are turned in on themselves do not have their share of misfortune. What I am saying is this, the more a person dwells on his or her bad luck or misfortune the more that person invites ill health—mentally and physically. It is when we become intentional about helping others that we become happier and healthier people.

In Mark's gospel, we have an account of Jesus healing a paralytic. Chapter two, verses one through six present to us an interesting account of the healing. The individuals involved are Jesus, the paralyzed man and, most importantly, four friends who make the healing possible. Without these friends to help, he could never have experienced the healing power of Jesus. Let's look at the scenario.

Jesus has concluded a tour of the Synagogues in the surrounding area and returned to Capernaum. Evidently, the news of his having healed others has preceded his coming back to Capernaum. Here is Jesus in a home. The crowd presses in, filling the house to capacity, overflowing out the doorway. Jesus is talking to the large crowd, when a smaller group appears, including four men who are carrying a paralyzed friend with them. Unable to get close to Jesus, they analyze what needs to be done. The roof of that house was flat, as were all the houses there in Palestine. They were often used as a place of quiet and rest. So, there was probably a crude ladder or outdoor stairway leading up to the roof, which consisted of flat wooden beams laid across from one wall to the other. These beams or rafters were usually spaced about three feet apart. That three-foot space was covered with small branches or brushwood packed tight with clay and covered over with a thin mixture of sand and clay.

It would have been quite easy for the four friends to dig out the filling between two of the beams. Such removal could have been repaired fairly easily. So these four friends did not lose much time hoisting their paralyzed friend to the rooftop.

They dug an opening and lowered their friend into the very presence of Jesus. Jesus, seeing their faith, said to the paralyzed man, "Son your sins are forgiven" (NRSV).

Jesus responded to the Jewish leaders who questioned his authority to forgive sins, "Which is easier to say...'Your sins are forgiven,' or to say 'stand up and walk'? But so that you may know that the Son of Man has authority on Earth to forgive sins," he said to the paralytic, "I say to you stand up, take your mat and go to your home." The people there were all amazed and glorified God, saying, "We have never seen anything like this" (NRSV)!

In this story, we find a wonderful example of what it means to help others and to be helped by others. As so often happens we don't know everything we would like to know about a Biblical story. Questions come to me. How long had these four guys known the paralytic? These four men possessed compassion and genuine concern for their friend. I'll bet they were in pretty good physical condition to be able to hoist him up on the roof and lower him to Jesus. They showed that they had faith. They had ingenuity and creativity. They possessed determination and boldness.

You and I may not have all of these attributes, but being a Christian, a follower of Jesus, we do possess a caring, concerned heart. When was the last time you did a random act of kindness? How did it make you feel? Within the last couple of weeks I've visited with two or three members of Lindenwood whom I have observed helping others.

An eighty-five-year-old man has been faithful in helping new, first time visitors feel at home. He offers worship bulletins and helps them find a place to sit. He visits with them before and following worship. So far as I know, he's never been a deacon. He just likes people and helping people.

"I really feel good about what I do. Getting to know people and making them feel good helps me to feel good." In the next breath, he said, "Did you know Walt is not doing good?" I worked with him years ago. He's a neat guy. This helper was more concerned about others than he was talking about himself.

A sixty-two year old man drives one of our buses, picking up people for church. "It's amazing how much the little things you do for others may mean to them. Last Sunday I picked up this little lady, and she said, 'I've been in the house all week, haven't seen a single person until you came today.'"

He said she talked with him all the way to church. When she got ready to get out of the bus, she smiled and said, "Thank you for talking to me. I probably talked you to death!"

"Oh no, I enjoyed it, too," he said. She leaned over and hugged him before she stepped down from his bus.

Both the eighty-five-year-old and the sixty-two-year-old enjoy good health, physically, mentally, and emotionally. I wonder how much it has to do with their outlook, their attitude?

Another man who worked out in the cold and heat helping members and visitors find parking places several years ago shared with me, "You'd be surprised how much it meant to our older members for me to find a place for them to park near the door."

Recently, Dot and I went shopping at a drug store on Summer Ave. It was drizzling rain when we parked our car. We noticed a young man, nice looking, waiting to catch a public transit bus. He had the collar of his coat pulled up trying to stay dry and warm.

When we came out of the store twenty-five minutes later, there he stood. It was a Saturday. We rolled our window down and asked if he needed our help. We were at Perkins and Summer. He was waiting for a bus to take him a mile or so east to White Station. We offered him a ride. He accepted. We took him to White Station; I hated to put him out in the rain.

We inquired his destination. It was about another mile south on White Station and then east on a side street. We took him to the house he indicated was his final destination—a nice looking, well kept home. He thanked us, saying he was going there to visit with his child. We told him were glad to help and invited him to Lindenwood.

He smiled real big. "Have a blessed day and thank you so much," he said as he walked away toward the house.

Dot and I were quiet as we started home. It was a good feeling, a warm feeling. Like the eighty-five-year-old and sixty-two-year-old, it was really not much on our part, but it did help someone who was hurting and in need.

Think about the story of the Good Samaritan. Do you think this was a random act of kindness? I don't believe it was. I think the Samaritan probably had been helping people for years. In my mind, I can see him growing up with loving, caring parents who encouraged him to have compassion on the less fortunate. His kind and caring act on the road to Jericho was no isolated incident in this Samaritan's life. He did what he did because he was the kind of man he was. He didn't get that way overnight. Over the years, he had cultivated the habit of helping others. I like to believe that he enjoyed a robust life with good health.

Thank God if you grew up in such an environment. If you have a desire to help others, it will serve as a medicine to bring healing and wholeness to others. It will also bring healing and wholeness to you. In spite of any ailments or infirmities, you may be plagued with, you will have what it takes to keep going. Your ailment or infirmity may not clear up. It may not be cured, but you will be healed, made whole. Your ailments will recede into nothingness.

Did you know there is a web site, < www.actsofkindness.org >, where people exchange ideas about practicing good deeds in their communities? They tell stories about the generosity they have received from or given to strangers.

One young mother went to a bank in New York City to withdraw some money from the cash machine. She had her two-year-old with her. The child kept pulling away from his mom, distracting her.

After leaving the bank, she went to a grocery store to shop. When she was checking out, she opened her purse and discovered she'd left her money in the money machine's dispenser. Heartsick, she returned to the bank. The money machine contained no money. She went to a bank officer and asked him to check and see if, in fact, she had withdrawn the money that day.

The bank officer asked for her debit card. He looked at the number on it and walked over to his desk. He came back with the money and handed it to her saying, "A kind man found your money and turned it in to me."

The lady praised God and said, "That man must be feeling really good by now."

The bank officer smiled and said, "I'm sure he is."

A study of people who volunteered on a regular basis to help others through acts of kindness revealed that, of the entire group, about 30% stated their health to be good when the study began. Sometime later that percentage had risen to forty-two! The time spent volunteering had a positive effect on the people's health.

A study of 1200 adults over age sixty-five showed that those participants who regularly volunteered to help others actually lived longer than those who were not volunteers.

Jesus said very clearly, "It is more blessed to give than to receive." (In Acts 20:35, NRSV, he is quoted saying this.)

By losing our lives, we find them. By giving our love and caring for others, we experience feelings of wholeness and health.

By practicing the art of forgetting self, we find joy and we overcome feelings of loneliness. Arthur Gordon, writer of stories for *Guideposts,* tells of taking a hike with two of his children through the hills of North Georgia. They came to a tiny cabin with a picket fence. Behind the fence was a white-haired mountain woman working in her garden. They stopped to admire the woman's flowers and learned that she lived there by herself, all alone.

One of Arthur Gordon's children asked the lady, "How do you keep from being lonesome?"

"Oh," she said, "if that feeling comes on me in summertime, I take a bunch of my flowers to a shut-in down the road. And if its winter, I just go out and feed the birds."

Acts of kindness and compassion—these were the antidote for loneliness. It made her forget her arthritic pains, too. They served to make her immune to self-pity.

In our first church up in Fayette County, there was Cousin Laura. She grew beautiful flowers, and each Sunday she carried a beautiful bouquet to the church and put them on the altar. She fed rabbits and kittens and stray dogs. I can't ever remember her complaining about physical ailments. She rode her horse about ten to twelve miles on her birthday every year, never worrying about her own physical condition. She did this until her mid 70's. She was a whole person.

A fifty-eight year old woman in Nashville has made an annual trip to East Tennessee Appalachia at Christmas time with vanloads of clothing and toys for people who live in old school buses and dig through the waste bins looking for food. She includes Bibles with her gifts. This fifty-eight-year-old has rheumatoid arthritis. She has had numerous surgeries on her back, neck, and feet, but she keeps going. She is not free of pain, but she is a whole person.

Several years ago, she was one of ten people or groups of people from across the country chosen as those who make a difference in the lives of those less fortunate. Her arthritic condition kept her from going to Washington D. C. to receive the honor and her award. She sent her parents. Today, she cannot do enough for her two children and grandchildren.

There is definitely something therapeutic about forgetting ourselves through helping others. Some people feel a calling to the helping professions; doctors, nurses, physical therapists, etc. About two years ago Dot and I met this wonderful woman at Faith Rehab. She had a special calling to minister to her patients through her genuine caring and loving ways. She is always upbeat and positive.

In my possession is a small book, 5" X 7", 1 ¼" thick. On pages 34-37 are listed the scout law. That law, is still a part of Scouting today, and reads, "A scout is trustworthy, loyal, helpful, friendly, courteous, kind, obedient, cheerful, thrifty, brave, clean, and reverent" (< www.scouting.org >). One of those laws that speaks to me more and more as I grow older is number three. "He must be prepared to help... He must do at least one good turn to somebody every day."

On page 26 of that old Boy Scout Handbook of mine is a list of suggested good turns, about 50 different ways to help others. That list is somewhat outdated (circa 1942). All in all, there are many things we can do to help others, if we really care.

If we work at responding affirmatively to other people's needs in endless small ways, we will find the healing power we need. Tenderness and compassion are just as important, if not more important than some medications or prescriptions.

Prayer

Dear God,

Make us ever sensitive to your many kindnesses to us. Help us to develop to its fullest our capacity to care for and help others. May we do the many small acts of kindness for others with no thought of recognition or accolade.

Give us the same caring spirit that the four friends of the paralytic possessed. Give us the sensitive, caring heart that the Good Samaritan had.

Help us to get outside of ourselves and focus on others that we may experience your wholeness and your holiness.

In the name of the Great Physician we pray.

Amen

The Role of Prayer in Healing
James 5:13-16, I Thessalonians 5:16-19

Does prayer heal?

Dr. Larry Dossey, well known medical doctor and pioneer in prayer and healing, had some most interesting and encouraging words to share in his book, *Healing Words* (1993).

During his residency training at a hospital in Dallas, Texas, he had his first patient with terminal cancer in both lungs. He explained to his patient the options for treatment and shared with him the fact that he, Dr. Dossey, thought that treatment would do very little good. So, the man received no treatment. Whenever Dossey stopped by his patient's bed, he was surrounded by visitors from his church singing and praying. Dossey thought to himself, "it won't be long 'til these friends will be singing and praying at his funeral."

A year later Dossey was working elsewhere when a colleague who was still at the hospital in Dallas called him and said, "Would you like to see your old patient?"

See him? Dossey couldn't believe the man was still alive. He went to the hospital, met his doctor friend, was shown the chest x-rays, and was totally stunned. The man's lungs were completely clear—no sign of cancer. Yet, the only therapy he had received was prayer.

Dossey shared all of this with two of his medical school professors. Neither was willing to believe that prayer could cause such a miraculous thing to occur.

Dossey himself had years ago given up the faith of his childhood. He had come to believe in the power of modern medicine. Prayer had seemed to him meaningless, so he dismissed the whole thing from his mind.

The years passed. He became Chief of Staff at a large urban hospital. He was aware that many of his patients used prayer, but he put little trust in it. Then, in late 1980 he began to come across studies that showed that prayer brings about significant changes in a variety of physical conditions. In one study, approximately 400 patients in a coronary unit of the San Francisco General Hospital were assigned to either a group that was prayed for by prayer groups or to a group that was not remembered in prayer. No one knew which group the patients were in.

Those praying were simply given the patients first names, along with brief descriptions of their medical problems. They were asked to pray each day until the patient was discharged from the hospital, but were given no instructions how to do it or what to say.

When the study was completed ten months later, the prayed for patients benefited in several significant areas:

- They were five times less likely to require antibiotics.
- They were 2.50 times less likely to suffer congestive heart failure.
- They were less likely to suffer cardiac arrest.

If the medical technique being studied had been a new drug or surgical procedure, it would probably have been heralded as a breakthrough. Even one hardboiled skeptic, A Dr. William Nolen, who had written a book questioning the validity of faith healing, acknowledged, "If this is a valid study, we doctors ought to be writing on our patients sheets 'pray three times a day.' If it works, it works."

In his research on prayer and healing, Dr. Dossey discovered studies that suggest that prayer can have a beneficial effect on high blood pressure, wounds, headaches, and anxiety.

In those studies, good results occurred, not only when people prayed for specific outcomes, but also when they prayed for a patient in general terms. A simple "according to Thy will, O God," the simple attitude of hopeful prayer or God's holy presence accompanied by genuine empathy, caring, and compassion seemed to set the stage for healing.

Love increases the power of prayer. Throughout the history of humankind the power of love to change things has been noted. "Love moves the flesh," as the blushing and palpitation experienced by lovers attest. Throughout history tender, loving care has been recognized as a valuable element in healing.

A survey of 10,000 men with heart disease found close to a 50% reduction in frequency of angina pains in those who perceived their wives as supportive and loving.

It is almost universal with healers who use faith and prayer that love is the power that makes it possible for them to reach out, to heal, even at a distance. The sincere feeling of warmth and caring is so pronounced that the one praying for healing, literally becomes one with the one being prayed for. Agnes Sanford, well-known figure in healing ministry had it right: "Only love can light the healing fire."

Dr. Dossey points out that, as a boy, he heard these words nonstop "pray unceasingly." Yet he was never successful in doing so. At night in bed he would pray and then find later he had fallen to sleep in the midst of praying. Dossey declares that "prayer never sleeps." The idea that prayer might occur in the depths of the unconscious, even during dreams, may seem preposterous. The possibility that our unconscious might know how to pray better than our conscious mind is simply not entertained.

A Dr. Herbert Benson of Harvard Medical School found that patients who prayed or were prayed for with simple mantras found healthful, physiological changes taking place in their bodies. "Lord Jesus Christ, have mercy upon me," "Shalom-shalom," "Our Father in Heaven," or "The Lord is My Shepherd"—these simple prayer mantras repeated many times each day caused healthful, physiological changes to take place.

Just praying a simple, open-ended prayer can be just as effective as precise pin pointed petitions: "Thy will be done (or according to Thy will)," "May the best thing happen." A spontaneous prayer like this brings positive results.

Dr. Dossey relates a patient of his who was dying. Dossey sat with the man and his family the day before he died. He knew he had little time left. The man chose his words carefully. He shared the fact that, although he had not been a religious person, he had begun to pray.

"What do you pray for," asked Dossey.

"It isn't for anything," said the man. "It reminds me that I am not alone."

Prayer causes healing. Prayer works miracles. Prayer reminds us that we are never alone.

As I indicated earlier, what I have shared with you so far was first printed in Dr. Larry Dossey's book, *Healing Words*, published in paperback in 1993 by Harper/San Francisco. I encourage you to try to secure a copy for yourself if it is still in print when you are reading this.

Reading, thinking about, and reflecting upon God's healing power in the lives of others will always strengthen your faith and enable you to become a more efficient prayer.

Hear now, some words about becoming a more effective intercessor as you pray for others. Here are some helpful thoughts from two prayer giants, William Russell Maltby and Douglas Van Steer. It was a blessed privilege for me to spend a week with Van Steer in 1987.

> I found that to pray for other people is a thing that cannot be hurried. It did not suffice; it was not real, to name a dozen names and ask God to bless them. Every name I found had to stand alone until it was the name of someone as real as me. I found that sincerity required me to be deliberate—one friend at a time. I found that I could not think of any of these, my friends, in the presence of God without some change coming over my thoughts, some stronger sense of their worth before God. (William Russell Maltby)

> Each person must learn to shape intercessory prayer after his or her own taste. I have found that hands are a wonderful symbol of giving. When someone takes my hand sincerely or puts a hand on my arm or on my shoulder, there is something special about what this body language is trying to tell me about the caring behind it. In intercessory prayer, I have often envisioned the nail-printed hand of Christ being laid upon the one I was praying for, and at the same moment the other pierced hand being laid on me. There is no form of prayer that is more obvious an act of real love than the costly act of intercessory prayer. Let us in our prayers for each join those who with Christ bear the burdens of creation. (Douglas V. Steer)

Benefit from these helpful, encouraging thoughts, ideas, and encouraging testimonies. Now, here are seven helpful hints on how to pray for your own healing.

These thoughts were first suggested by Rev. John H. Parke, The Order of St. Luke the Physician.

1. Realize

Know that you were born for a glorious, triumphant and whole life, that the will of God for you is good, that the Great Physician wills wholeness for you.

2. Repent

Not all illness is caused by sin, but usually somewhere, somehow, a physical or moral law of the universe has been broken, willfully or accidentally, either by you or by someone closely affecting your life. Insofar as you may have been at fault, confession and a sincere desire to change is needed. Where another may be responsible, your forgiveness of that person is required (Mark 11:25-26; James 5:16, NRSV). Put away all hostility toward conditions, circumstances, persons, places, and things.

3. Relax

Consciously release all the tensions of your body, all the doubts and anxieties of your mind. Lay aside all criticism, prejudices, and preconceived notions, and keep an open mind. Let go and let God.

4. Visualize Perfect Health

Reverse the negative patterns of disease, limitation, and troubles. Do not syndicate your ills and complaints. Using your imagination, see yourself the way you believe God wants you to be—perfect wholeness in every part of your being—body, mind and spirit. Visualize Jesus, the Great Physician, reaching forward to touch you. As you feel His touch, know that His healing power is flowing within you.

5. Ask

And you shall receive (Matthew 7:7, NRSV). "Whatsoever ye shall ask in my name, that will I do" (John 14:13, NRSV). Ask with faith—"Lord, I believe" (Mark 9:24, NRSV). "Believe that you have received it, and it will be yours"

(Mark 11:24, NRSV). Ask with thanksgiving—"Father, I thank thee that thou hast heard me" (John 11:41, NRSV). Even before any results are evident, start thanking God that his healing power is at work. Ask with joy—"Jesus, I praise you. Jesus, I love you"—just pour out your heart in praise and love to him.

6. Accept

Let God touch every area of your life with his power. Realize God's presence continually. Live in the now, think in the now, and act in the now. Live in a constant state of expectancy of God's constant adequacy.

7. Do Something in Response to Your Healing

Do something that you could not do before. Do something for someone else who needs you. Do something special for God. Witness to all what God has done for you.

A Healing Prayer for the World

Let the rain come and wash away the ancient grudges, the bitter hatreds held and nurtured over generations. Let the rain wash away the memory of the hurt, the neglect. Then let the sun come out and fill the sky with rainbows. Let the warmth of the sun heal us wherever we are broken. Let it burn away the fog so that we can see each other clearly. So that we can see beyond labels, beyond accents, gender or skin color. Let the warmth and brightness of the sun melt our selfishness. So that we can share the joys and feel the sorrows of our neighbors. And let the light of the sun be so strong that we will see all people as our neighbors. Let the earth, nourished by rain, bring forth flowers to surround us with beauty. And let the mountains teach our hearts to reach upward to heaven. Amen (Rabbi Harold S. Kushner)

Prayer.

Loving God,
We thank you for these encouraging words by medical doctors, prayer giants, and a Rabbi. Help us to hold on to the encouragement we have received. Help us to pass it on to those we are praying for.

Love Brings Better Health
I Corinthians 13:4-7, 13, I John 3:11-14

Health and wholeness are enhanced when one feels loved, truly and deeply loved. On the other hand those who do not feel loved or who feel all alone in the world have more difficulty with health problems and wholeness as a person.

Studies have revealed that those who are in a meaningful relationship with at least one human being experience greater joy. Their happiness in that relationship strengthens their immune system. It helps them when adversity comes into their lives.

Three true stories illustrate the point I am trying to make:

A pastor of a church in a small town tells about the most passionate person he had ever known. Gladys was her name. She was a retired schoolteacher. She lived with her only child, a daughter. She was extremely happy. Her life was fulfilled. She felt deeply loved by her daughter, and she shared her happiness and fulfillment with everyone she met.

Gladys loved everybody, and everybody loved her. When a new baby arrived, so did a homemade doll from Gladys. When a person went into the hospital, they soon received a card saying that Gladys was praying for them. She was seventy years old herself, but she visited, as she said, "the old folks who needed company."

When you were not feeling well, homemade soup from Gladys' kitchen was a medicine that seemed to always work. Everybody in Franklin County, Kentucky loved Gladys (except the chickens).

Then something terrible happened. Gladys had a confrontation with her daughter. Before it could be resolved the younger woman packed up all her things and moved out. It was a crushing blow to Gladys. She was never the same. She sent no more notes to the living, no more flowers to the dead. She made no more visits to her neighbors, nor did she invite any of the neighbors into her home.

Evidently, this dear woman had been so deeply hurt by her daughter that she made certain she would never be hurt again.

She ended all personal relationships. These drastic changes in her life did her in. Somehow, if she had had a deep personal love for Christ Jesus and she had felt God's unconditional love for herself, she may have survived this tragic turn of events in her life.

No matter what Gladys tried, nothing worked. Within a short period of time, Gladys was dead. She died of a broken heart.

John, The Apostle of Love, writes in Chapter 3 of his first letter, "For this is the message which you have heard from the beginning, that we should love one another... He who does not love abides in death." (Vs10, 14b, NRSV).

A Dr. James Lynch wrote a book entitled *The Broken Heart: The Consequences of Loneliness*. In it, he makes this statement: "Whether it be heart disease, cancer, alcoholism, or whatever, the mortality rate for those who are socially isolated and deprived of meaningful human contacts is five times greater than those who do have someone to love them."

When one is not loved, the will to live is drastically diminished. The story of Gladys is a classic example.

Now, the story of another woman who continued to cope in spite of a lack of touch and hugs from her children:

She lived a life of deep love with her husband of many years. Her every physical need was being met, but she was lonely after he died. Donna Swanson wrote a poignant poem entitled "Minnie Remembers," explaining the need for touch and hugging.

> "God,
> My hands are old.
> I've never said that out loud before
> But they are.
> I was so proud of them once.
> They were soft
> Like the velvet smoothness of a firm, ripe
> Peach.
> Now the softness is more like worn-out sheets
> or withered leaves.
> When did these slender, graceful hands
> Become gnarled, shrunken claws?"

The speaker of the poem continues to question God about where the old hands came from and where the young ones went. She says the old hands remind her of her "worn-out body." Then she turns to the topic of touch.

"How long has it been since someone touched me?
Twenty years?
Twenty years I've been a widow."

As a widow, the speaker of the poem acknowledges that she was respected, smiled at, but alone.

"But never touched.
Never held so close that loneliness
was blotted out."

The widow reminisces about when she was young, when her own mother held her, comforted her, and cared for her. She recalls her first kiss by a boy and the senses it stirred. Then, she reflects on her husband and children. She speaks of her life with her husband raising the kids, and growing old together.

"And, God, Hank didn't seem to mind
if my body thickened and faded a little.
He still loved it. And touched it.
And we didn't mind if we were no longer beautiful.
And the children hugged me a lot.
O God, I'm lonely!

"God, why didn't we raise the kids to be silly
and affectionate as well as
dignified and proper?
You see, they do their duty.
They drive up in their fine cars;
They come to my room to pay their respects.
They chatter brightly, and reminisce.
But they don't touch me.
The call me "Mom" or "Mother"
or "Grandma."

"Never Minnie,
My mother called me Minnie.
So did my friends.
Hank called me Minnie, too.

But they're gone.
And so is Minnie.
Only Grandma is here.
And God! She's lonely!'"

Here we have the perfect example of just how important touching, hugging, and holding are for all human beings. A measure of well-being and wholeness depends on our experiencing genuine love, caring, and unselfish love. Those who are growing old: parents and loved ones, especially those living alone or in nursing homes, need love expressed physically.

In one of our homilies, I quoted a person as saying "Love is the spark that lights the flame of healing." I firmly believe this to be true.

Now, a third true story—almost unbelievable, but true nevertheless. A famous plastic surgeon had a visit from a woman who said, "It's my husband. He was injured in a fire. He tried to save his parents from a burning house, but he couldn't get to them. They both perished. His face was burned and badly disfigured, and he has given up on life. He has gone into hiding and won't let anyone see him, not even me. He has shut me, and everyone else, completely out of his life."

"Don't worry," the doctor responded, "I can fix him. With the great advances we've made in plastic surgery in recent years, I can restore his face."

"But that's just it," said the woman. "He won't let anyone help him. He thinks God did this to him to punish him because he didn't save his parents." Then came her shocking words, "Dr. I want you to disfigure my face so I can look like him! If I can share in his pain, maybe then he will let me back into his life. I love him so much. I want so much to be with him. And if that's what it takes, that's what I want to do, disfigure my face."

Of course, the plastic surgeon would not agree. Moved deeply by the wife's determined and total love, with the wife's permission, he went to the man's room and knocked, but there was no answer. He then said loudly through the door, "I know you are in there and I know you can hear me. I'm a plastic surgeon, and I want you to know I can restore your face."

No response. The doctor pleaded, "Please come out, and let me help you."

Still no answer. Then still speaking through the door, the doctor told the man what his wife was asking him to do. "She wants me to make her face look like yours in the hope that you will let her back into your life. That's how much she loves you. That's how much she wants to help you!"

There was a brief moment of silence. Then, ever so slowly, the doorknob began to turn...and the disfigured man came out to make a new beginning and to find a new life. By her total love, he was set free, brought out of hiding, and given a new start.

Gladys' life ended in tragedy. Here was a dear soul who once felt and shared deep love. So long as she felt her daughter's love she was empowered to love others, to help bring healing and wholeness to people of all ages, in all circumstances in her small town. But once the flow of love into her life was cut off by the horrible conflict and confrontation, her life dried up. So severe was that experience that she lost all desire to live. The words of John, The Apostle of Love, proved to be true. "He (or she) who does not love abides in death" (NRSV).

On one occasion Jesus said, "He who loves his Mother or Father more than me is not worthy of me" (Matthew 10:37, NRSV). Who knows, if both Gladys and her daughter had loved Jesus and experienced his love for them they would both have had a reservoir of love and strength to draw upon. Their confrontation could have been resolved. Their lives could have returned to rich, productive, healthy states of being.

Minnie knew love. She had known it through her husband, Hank, for many years. She had probably known it through her children when they were younger. But somehow, little by little the children became preoccupied with other things, material things. They somehow forgot the importance of love, physical touching, and verbal expressions. I don't know how Minnie's story ended. Hopefully, she found her need for hugging and physical caressing fulfilled. Hopefully someone who tended to her there in the extended care or nursing home sensed her loneliness and longing and alerted Minnie's children so that her very last days were love-filled, healing and wholeness returning to her heart.

The loving wife who was willing to undergo horrible disfigurement for her husband's sake is the shining example of the power of love to heal.

I don't know where you are in terms of knowing that you are loved. I do know this. When I am aware of God's love for me, the Christian love of others for me, I cope with problems much better. Minor annoyances disappear, and major problems don't seem so overwhelming. I am suggesting to you and to myself that we become very intentional about cultivating love, Christian love, and agape love with our families and our circle of friends in the world. Not only will it bring joy, it will enhance your health and increase your awareness of being a whole person.

Prayer

Loving God.

Help us to draw deeply from your unconditional love so that we may be channels of blessings for others, families, friends, and strangers alike.

Amen.

The three stories in this chapter were told by Maxie Dunnam in his workbook *Loving the Jesus Way*. Used by permission.

The Healing Power of Positive Thoughts
Philippians 4:8-18 Proverbs 17:22

We have within us this tremendous power. By controlling what we think about and what we allow to enter our minds, we can to some degree, control our lives, including our health. Not only is this true, it is also true that we can have an influence on the lives, including the health, of others; our family, our closest friends.

It is important then for us to spend time filling our minds with positive thoughts. Paul said to the Christians at Philippi, "Whatsoever things are honest, true, just and lovely, think on these things" (Philippians 4:8, NRSV).

The Message, a translation by Eugene H. Peterson, reads this way. "You'll do best by filling your minds and meditating on things that are true, noble, authentic, gracious, the best, not the worst; the beautiful, not the ugly; things to praise, not things to curse."

The writer of Proverbs said, "A cheerful heart is good medicine, but a downcast spirit dries up the bones" (NRSV). *Moffatt's Translation* renders this 22nd verse of Proverbs 17 in this manner, "A glad heart helps and heals." Several of the Proverbs speak of the importance of thinking positively and remaining cheerful, cultivating a cheerful attitude. They indicate that a dividend or blessing in doing so is better health. It is important then for us to avoid becoming negative, down-in-the-mouth people.

Leonard Sweet, in his book, *The Jesus Prescription for a Healthy Life*, encourages his readers to avoid doing those things that cause stress, unhappiness and poor health. He lists what he calls the 10 Commandments of Stress. I have chosen certain ones to make my point.

1. Thou shalt wear a grim expression at all times.
3. Thou shalt cram and store all of thy negative feelings in thy gut (stomach).
7. Thou shalt not party (celebrate).
8. Thou shalt not take a vacation.
9. Thou shalt expect the worst in all situations, blaming everyone around thyself for everything and dwelling on the feebleness, the faults, and fears of others.

10. Thou shalt try to be in control of all things at all times, no matter what.

Have you known people who fit this category? Have there been times when you, yourself have been guilty of a negative approach to life?

It will help us in relationships and in our own sense of well being if we work at following Paul's words to the Philippians or the writer of Proverbs regarding a cheerful heart. We need to always take our responsibilities in life seriously, but at the same time, guard against taking ourselves too seriously. In my years of life as I look back on it, I have been guilty at times of taking myself too seriously. Therefore it pleased me to no end to receive a Father's Day card just recently wherein a dear one wrote these words, "Two things that I adore about you; First, your deep tenderness and caring and second, your delightful personality of timeless youthfulness. You are a joy..."

In all humility, I can say I have always tried to be this kind of person. In all honesty, I must say I have failed at both at times. But more often, I have failed at remaining cheerful and youthful in my outlook. In other words, I have taken myself too seriously. By the grace of God, it is my desire to always have a cheerful heart, filling my mind with things that are the best, the beautiful, the things that cause me to praise God.

Leonard Sweet in his book, mentioned above, includes what he calls qualities of childlike persons. They will "walk in the rain, jump in mud puddles, collect rainbows, stop along the way, build sand castles, watch the moon and stars come out, say hello to everyone. They will go barefoot, go on adventures, sing in the shower, have a merry heart, read children's books, get silly, take bubble baths, get new sneakers, hold hands, hug and kiss, and dance."

If we are to avoid becoming a person who sends out negative vibes to others we will practice some of these childlike behaviors. None of us wants to be the type of person who sends out negative waves to others. We don't intentionally desire to affect others with a negative, down-in-the-mouth attitude. As I stated in the opening sentences of this homily, "we have within us this tremendous power to determine our own outlook on life, and to some degree, control our health, mentally, spiritually, and physically. Also, we have the power to influence the health and happiness of others: family and close friends."

By God's grace we will send out positive, hope-filled vibes or waves of energy that inspire others to think well of themselves and remain healthy.

It is a proven fact that there is this "field of spiritual energy" around each one of us. Every person we relate to has to deal with that energy force of ours. We can emit a positive energy that inspires others and helps them remain healthy, or we can emit a negative energy that tends to make others weak or listless, sapping their strength.

I sincerely believe that every follower of Christ should desire to send out or emit a positive, helpful energy force that will help others. If we will practice thinking about and meditating on those things that are noble, uplifting, beautiful, and praise worthy in the eyes of Christ, we will be for all people a ray of hope, a source of joy.

I don't believe that anyone in their right mind, their God-given mind, would intentionally want to be otherwise. And yet, we all probably know of at least one person who is always negative, always down-in-the-mouth. Common sense tells us to avoid those people as much as possible.

Let me give you an example of how other people can adversely affect your life and your health. In this case, it was not negative mental or spiritual vibes; it was a negative habit that caused sickness and poor health for someone dear and close to the person who caused it.

One of my uncles who smoked cigarettes and cigars incessantly, constantly, for thirty or forty years emitted or sent out very harmful fumes into the air at home, in his car, as well as outdoors. Back in those days, I suppose no one realized the harmful effects of second-hand smoke. The second-hand smoke lingered in the air in their home and in their car. As a result, his wife was exposed to those harmful fumes. She had to go to the old St. Joseph Hospital (where St. Jude is today). She had an upper lobe of one of her lungs removed, all of this the result of something someone else had done, not something she had caused.

If this occurs on the physical level, can you see the same thing occurring at the spiritual or mental level?

It happens! If we allow negative, ugly thoughts to permeate our minds and hearts, those will be the very things that we send out to others. Those negative harmful thoughts may not necessitate surgery, but they can result in poor health for ourselves and for others, mentally and physically. They will necessitate our examining our lives and removing by choice the harmful thoughts and attitudes we have allowed in us.

Let us learn to develop a cheerful heart. Some of us may say, "I'm just not by nature the optimistic type. I should not be expected to serve the Lord or others with gladness." But the spirit of cheerfulness is not something that is automatic. Cultivating a cheerful outlook on life is as much a deliberate act as is the attempt to control one's temper, or the determination to be compassionate toward people in need. The good medicine of a cheerful heart cannot be the result of a pharmacist mixing chemicals or ingredients and encasing them in a capsule to be swallowed. It is the product of a will that refuses to give way to gloom.

It is the product of a person smiling or laughing at least three times a day and once before going to bed regardless of the events or circumstances of that day. In addition to filling our minds with positive, upbeat, inspiring reading materials on a regular basis, we could practice Leonard Sweet's childlike behaviors:

> Fly kites, laugh, and cry, ask lots of questions, give up worrying and guilt, talk with animals, look at the sky, stay up late, climb trees, take naps, do nothing, day dream, play with toys, have pillow fights, learn new stuff, get excited about everything, be a clown, listen to music, do anything else that brings more happiness. Celebrate, relax, communicate, love, create.

Make it a habit of yours to: "Frequent beaches, meadows, mountain tops, swimming pools, forests, playgrounds, picnic areas, birthday parties, circuses, cookie shops, ice cream parlors, theaters, aquariums, zoos, museums, planetariums, toy stores, festivals, and other places where children of all ages come to play..." And remember, "It's never too late to have a happy childhood!" (p 66, 67, *The Jesus Prescription for a Healthy Live*).

Let me add, it's never too late to cultivate a cheerful heart and a positive, upbeat energy field to emit to others, especially to our family and friends at work or at church.

Let me suggest that one way to be sure you are emitting positive, inspiring energy is to keep a daily record of your interactions, conversations, with the people who are put in your path that day: a clerk at the fast food restaurant, an attendant at the gas station, the drivers of other cars near yours at traffic lights or stop signs, the bank clerk, the cashier at the grocery store or pharmacy, the server at the restaurant, the person who waits on you at the service department where your car is maintained, or the ticket counter at the airport or the flight attendant, your spouse, your children... Writing down in your notebook at end of the day your role in each relationship, give yourself 5 stars for every time you encouraged someone or affirmed them verbally or non-verbally. What was your demeanor? What kind of energy did you share with others?

Hopefully we did not wear a grim expression. Hopefully we did not expect the worst in every situation, blaming others for everything that went wrong. Hopefully we did not try to control every situation and every person we encountered that day.

By God's grace and a little determination on our part, we will radiate to others a cheerful heart, a genuine medicine for better health.

Prayer

Loving God,

We desire to be your instruments for healing. Infuse us with your spirit so that we radiate inspiration and hope and love to those around us each day. Help us to emit rays of encouragement to those who are hurting. Help us to remain childlike in our outlook on life so that we can enjoy life more and help others to do the same.

Amen.

The Ultimate Healing Experience
John 11: 20–25

Our scripture comes from John, Chapter 11.

The Setting: A small village just a few miles from Jerusalem Two sisters and a brother live there, Mary, Martha and Lazarus. It is a family who loves Jesus dearly. It is a home where Jesus must have felt secure and warmly cared for.

Lazarus is ill. Mary and Martha send a messenger. "Lord, the one you love is ill" (NRSV) Jesus: "His sickness won't end in death. It will bring glory to God and to His Son" (NRSV). Now, Jesus loved these siblings, but he remained where he was for two more days. Then he said to his disciples, "Now...we will go back to Judea (Bethany)" (NRSV). He explains that their friend is dead. To paraphrase, he says, "I am glad that we were detained. It is all designed so that you may come to believe! Now, you will have a chance to put your faith in me. Let's go to him!"

They arrive in Bethany, but Lazarus has been dead in the tomb for four days. Martha gets the word that Jesus has arrived.

"Lord if you had been here my brother would not have died. Yet even now I know that God will do anything you ask" (NRSV).

"I am the resurrection and the life. Those who believe in me, even though they die, will live," said Jesus. "I am the one who raises the dead to life! Everyone who has faith in me will live, even if (when) they die" (NRSV).

Jesus loves this family so dearly that, seeing their grief, Jesus begins to cry (vs 35, NRSV). Jesus goes to the tomb, tells the people, "roll the stone away," open the tomb.

Martha: "But Lord, Lazarus has been dead four days. There will be a horrible odor."

Jesus: "Didn't I tell you that if you have faith, you will see the glory of God."

The stone is then rolled away. Jesus looks up to heaven and prays, "Father, I thank you for answering my prayer." He said this for benefit of those looking on. Then the command, "Lazarus come out." It happened. Jesus said, "Remove the remnants of the burial cloths and let him go" (vs 44, NRSV). What a miracle!

Jesus, here in John 11, shows that He has the resurrection power, the ultimate power that defeats what we call death. Jesus is our source of the ultimate healing. Jesus, himself, drew upon that power when his own body was placed in a borrowed tomb and that's what we celebrate on Easter—from sunrise to sunset. Resurrection power!

As Christians, we understand that the death of our physical bodies is the process we go through in order to experience the ultimate healing! Death itself does not heal. Rather, death is a transition. It is a changing from one form to another. It is a transition to more life, to perfect wholeness, to ultimate health, to complete harmony with God.

As Christians, we claim all the promises of Jesus, including his promise of a glorious life beyond death. His ultimate promise in our scripture is, "I am the resurrection and the life. Those who believe in me will live, even though they die" (NRSV).

The basis we have for this ultimate healing is: (1) the incarnation—God living in Jesus of Nazareth, (2) the crucifixion, the physical death of Jesus (3) His resurrection. Without this assurance, this faith, this hope, all other healing is just a temporary alleviation or relief of a symptom. That's all. But in light of the resurrection and ascension, all other healing is a sneak preview of the ultimate healing.

"We're going to be changed into His likeness, have a body like His glorious body! Our eyes won't need glasses! Our knees and hips won't ache with arthritis. Our tongues won't gossip. We're going to have a resurrected body like that of Jesus following the resurrection morning" (Tommy Tyson).

It is important for us to remember that our creator God purposely did not design the human body to last forever. Physical death is an inescapable reality for each one of us.

Under the best possible conditions and circumstances, a human being might on rare occasions live to fulfill these words found in Genesis 6:3, "My spirit shall not abide in mortals forever, for they are flesh. Their days shall be one hundred twenty years" (NRSV).

Modern medical science can keep a human organism functioning indefinitely. The blood flow, the heartbeat may go on and on and on, even when signs of real life have long since ceased to function and brain waves have gone flat. How sad we cannot accept and truly believe that life beyond that moment we call death is the ultimate gift from God, A quality of life beyond our fondest dreams, perfect wholeness, and complete harmony with God and with all others.

Let me repeat—all physical healing is temporary. Even a miraculous healing like Lazarus' did not give him unending physical health here. Eventually he died.

> Due to the aging process (a part of God's plan for all of us) it is only a matter of time before another malfunction or breakdown of the physical system occurs. Eventually the human body does not respond to any kind of therapy. However, when this "container" in which we live is hopelessly flawed, depleted, worn out, the contents can be wonderfully whole.
>
> *(An Adventure in Healing & Wholeness*, pp. 54-58)

Paul, the Apostle sheds light on our understanding of death: "So we do not lose heart, even though our outer nature is wasting away, our inner nature is being renewed day by day. For this slight, momentary affliction is preparing us for an eternal weight of glory beyond all measure" (II Cor. 4 16-18, NRSV). Is Paul thinking about death as a slight, momentary affliction? Is he talking about that eternal measure of glory as a resurrected body? I believe he is. We who believe and accept for ourselves Jesus' promise have no doubt that a whole being ultimately healed is what we carry into life beyond this life.

Paul gave this entire issue his best thinking. Hear his words from I Corinthians 15:50, 55, and 57. From *The Message*:

> Why do you think I keep risking my life in this dangerous work (of preaching Christ and Him crucified, resurrected and alive)? Do you think that I'd keep doing this if I wasn't convinced of your resurrection and mine as guaranteed by the resurrected Jesus Christ, the Messiah?
>
> It's resurrection, resurrection, resurrection, always resurrection that undergirds what I do and say and the way I live! If there is no resurrection, we just eat, drink, work and then die. But don't fool yourselves. Don't be misled by those who doubt or question the resurrection.

Some skeptic is sure to ask, "How does resurrection work? Show me how, draw me a picture, give me a diagram, and explain it in detail."

Well, there are no diagrams or pictures for this new body, this transition that leads to perfect wholeness, ultimate health, and complete harmony with God. But there is an analogy or parallel experience to be found in gardening.

You plant a dead, dormant seed. Soon, there is new life, entirely different from the seed you planted. There is no visual likeness between seed and plant. You would never guess what a tomato, or a pumpkin, or a cucumber would look like by examining their seeds. What we plant in the soil and what grows out of it look nothing alike.

The dead body that is placed beneath the soil has no resemblance to the resurrected body that God will give us, that body that is glorified, ultimately healed, and made whole.

Once there was a boy in high school, a great athlete. His father was blind. Even so, the father never missed a game. His wife or one of their younger children would sit with the father and verbally describe what was happening. "Jimmy caught a pass, he made a touchdown, he kicked a field goal." The boy was truly a great athlete, one of the stars of his school's football team. It happened that the father had a massive heart attack and died the day of one of the final games of the season. The coach along with others did everything to comfort the boy. It would have been quite understandable had the boy not played that night, but that was not the case.

The boy hugged his mother and with tears in his eyes said, "Just think, mom, dad will see every play tonight. No one will have to describe anything to dad again—ever."

The father had experienced the ultimate healing, by making the transition from a limited physical body to a perfect resurrected body.

This is our faith, a simple childlike, trusting faith in a God who loves and heals. Hear these words:

I looked over Jordan and what did I see
comin' for to carry me home?
A band of angels comin' after me,

comin' for to carry me home.

If you get there before I do,
tell all my friends I'm a comin' too,
comin' for to carry me home.
I'm sometimes up
and sometimes down.
But still my soul feels heavenly bound,
comin' for to carry me home.
(African American Spiritual)

Precious Lord, take my hand,
lead me on, let me stand.
I am tired, I am weak, I am worn.
Through the storm, through the night,
lead me on to the light
Take my hand, precious Lord, lead me home.
(Thomas A. Dorsey, 1932)

These don't sound like the words of someone doubting that there is healing and wholeness on the other side of death.

Jesus was simple and straightforward in His teachings. Somehow, in my own simplistic approach to life and faith, I have a bit of sympathy for those who find satisfaction or peace only if they can reason everything out. These are the ones who absolutely must comprehend or perish. Their minds must be satisfied with complete understanding, especially when it comes to something like the resurrection and the ultimate healing experience. I graduated magna cum laude from seminary. But I must confess my greatest joy is to find God in simple things and people of simple faith.

Swing down chariot, stop and let me ride.
Swing down chariot, stop and let me ride.
Rock me Lord, rock me Lord, rock me easy—
I got a home on the other side.

Some glad morning when this life is 'ore,
I'll fly away.
To a home on God's celestial shore,
I'll fly away.

I'll fly away, oh glory. I'll fly away!
When I die, Hallelujah, bye and bye,
I'll fly away.

Why don't you swing down chariot, stop and let me ride
Swing down chariot, stop and let me ride.

I want to meet that great physician face to face and be made whole, forever and ever. I sincerely believe that we will.

Christian Healing Through the Centuries
Matthew 9:35-38, Acts 10:34-38

Jesus' ministry was so involved with healing that if you took a copy of the four Gospels and cut out or deleted every mention of healing or the casting out of demons, all you would have left would be a shambles of paper lace.

In the second and third centuries, healing was a taken-for-granted, integral part of Christianity. Justin Martyr, in writing to the Roman senate and the emperor argued the case for Christianity by pointing out how Christians, in the name of Jesus Christ, drove out demons and healed people when no one else could do so.

In the first three hundred years, Christians had a burning, deep faith in Jesus Christ, his power, and his Lordship. Nominal or casual Christians—"lukewarm" Christians—were the exceptions.

In A.D. 313, the Emperor Constantine declared Christianity legal and acceptable. The impact of this on the church was vast. It had numerous repercussions, actions, and reactions. Churches were flooded with people who were Christians in name only. Their faith and commitment to Christ left much to be desired.

A number of devout followers of Christ moved to the desert areas and started what we know as monasticism; the life style that included self-denial and deep commitment to Christ, his teachings, and his simple, servant-like way of life, including a deep faith in healing. Among the most fascinating Christians who went into the deserts around Egypt and Palestine were three men and a woman, all born in Cappadocia, in Eastern Asia Minor. The four were Basil, Gregory of Nazianzus, Gregory's brother and his sister Macrina.

Basil (c. 330, c. 379) was educated at Cappadocia, Caesarea, Constantinople, and Athens in the finest schools available at that time.

In 370, he was appointed Bishop of Caesarea. He founded and maintained a public hospital near Caesarea. He believed in the healing power of Christ, but he also believed in turning to the medical expertise that existed in that day. He felt that medicine was in keeping with the healing power of Christ, since medical science was given to us by God. Therefore, to reject the benefits of medicine would show a contentious spirit.

Macrina, one of the four, founded a Monastery for men and women on the family estate. Her brother, Gregory, was so impressed by his sister's life that he decided to write her biography. Gregory let it be known that he desired to include in the biography true stories or anecdotes about his sister and her life. A Roman soldier let it be known that he and his wife had visited Macrina at her monastery. He went to the men's quarters while his wife and little girl went to the women's quarters. The little girl had a badly infected eye. It was swollen and discolored.

Macrina took the child in her arms and kissed her eye saying, "Do me a favor and stay for dinner. I will give you some medicine for your daughter."

So they stayed and after dinner departed. Halfway home the mother said, "Oh, I forgot the medicine for our daughter's eye." Then turning toward the child she exclaimed, "But look, the eye is healed! Macrina gave us a cure from her faith and prayers and it has already healed." There was no sign of the infection or discoloration.

It is true today; spiritual healing has to do with the connection of body and soul. Healing comes about through the action of the living Christ within us.

Down through the ages, Christ has dwelt in the hearts and minds of those who have sought him out, invited him in, those who have given deep thought to his words, those who have sincerely longed for and hungered for his touch on their lives. He has healed and made whole those who trust him, and those who faithfully meet him at the table of Holy Communion.

Another Church father, Cyprian, writing in the third Century, said that Baptism itself could be one of the means whereby a person is healed. Also, the Eucharist, Holy Communion, was a major source of healing for the early church. It was the center or focal point or primary agent of healing. The bread and the wine were consecrated by the presiding liturgist to become the healing presence of Christ. In addition, oil, probably olive oil, was offered up with the bread and wine with this prayer, "Sanctify this oil, O God, grant health to those who use it."

The oil was used at church, in worship services for healing. It could also be carried into the homes of the sick by a priest or a layperson. The sick person would kneel for the laying on of hands.

He or she would then be anointed with the oil on the throat, the chest, the back and more liberally where the pain was the greatest. Prayers of thanksgiving were prayed. The patient was instructed to pray for his/her own recovery, also to make confession for sins. Following this, Holy Communion was partaken of. It was not unusual for a priest or a layperson or a group of them to return to the sick person's home every week until they were better. In the anointing and laying on of hands, the healing power of Christ was asked for.

An interesting aspect of healing in those early years was the act of exorcism—casting out of demons or evil spirits. By the third century, it was a common experience. Even the home of a sick person was exorcised before healing prayers were offered in that home.

Some theologians today consider those demons or evil spirits to be the same as what we consider neuroses or mental illnesses. If this is true then we might well pray for ourselves to be delivered from nagging, negative thoughts that impede our becoming a whole person. We are all neurotic in some sense.

Well, as Avery Brook points out in her excellent article in *Weavings, a Journal of the Christian Spiritual Life* (July/August 1991), "We all need to get rid of demons."

By the time of St. Augustine (354-430 A.D.), healings seemed to be fewer. Many Christians no longer practiced healing. Augustine, himself in his earliest writings said that the church should not continue to look for healings to occur. But, years later, just before his death he modified his earlier statement saying that although healings did not happen as often, they did in fact occur.

Avery Brook, in her research, points out that by the years 590-604 A.D. "civilization was falling apart." Even devout Christians had a gloomy outlook on life. Gregory the Great, Pope at that time, viewed sickness as a discipline sent from God.

What a contrast from the earliest years of the church! In those times, God was seen as the giver of health and wholeness. Now, barely 600 years later, there was a complete reversal of theology. It was a time of catastrophic disasters. Several large cities ceased to exist. Commercial life around the Mediterranean stopped. Education ground to a halt.

Christians couldn't wrap their minds around all of this. A happy and healthy life was no longer expected. The most you could think about and hope for was paradise after you left this world.

By the ninth and tenth centuries the ministry of healing for physical and emotional illnesses was largely forgotten. Then by the Age of Enlightenment (the seventeenth and eighteenth centuries), the totally rational approach had taken over both the Catholic and Protestant faiths. Yet, in spite of these official theological and liturgical positions of the church, healing continued with both Catholics and Protestants.

The Catholics experienced a resurgence of interest in pilgrimages to healing shrines, the most famous of which is Lourdes. Among Protestants, healings also continued. George Fox (1624-1691) and John Wesley (1703-1791) were leaders. Both wrote of healings through prayer for the sick. In 1842, a Lutheran pastor prayed for a woman severely ill with mental disorders. After a long spiritual battle she got better. People began to flock to this pastor's church for prayer and healing. Lutheran authorities became alarmed, and in 1846, forbade this pastor (Johann Blumhardt) to practice physical healing. His reply was that it was impossible for him to be the pastor and not have healings to just happen. The authorities were persuaded, and he was allowed to continue with a healing ministry.

Meanwhile, in 1851 in Switzerland, a young Swiss florist began praying for some co-workers who were ill and whose illnesses had not responded to medical treatment. She prayed for them and anointed them with oil. They were healed instantaneously! Other people who were in need of healing flocked to her. Eventually she was brought to trial for practicing medicine without a license. She won the trial. The publicity brought even more people to her for healing.

Moving into the turn of the century 1890's-1900's, we find a tremendous change in the attitude toward healings. This time individuals and churches more and more dedicated themselves to healing ministries. At first, it was outside what some call the mainline Protestant denominations and the Orthodox Catholic bodies.

It was in Pentecostal churches where the center of healing ministries was found. Many Christians found healing and speaking in strange languages objectionable, while others were drawn to them. They brought these experiences into their own denomination and congregation. The ministry of healing found its way into many mainline Protestant bodies, and the Catholic Church while the speaking in tongues was dropped or ignored.

Following WW II, four people who were involved in healing ministries stand out, William Branham, Oral Roberts, Kathryn Kuhlman, and Agnes Sanford. These four made major impacts on the credibility of healing. Branham in 1951, healed U. S. Congressman William Upshaw, who had been crippled since birth.

Oral Roberts was healed of TB and a stammer in speech in 1935. He worked closely with doctors, and in 1981, established the City of Faith Medical and Research Center.

All four of these leaders in the healing ministry of the twentieth century believed that healing was God's work and not their own. Kathryn Kuhlman especially did not like being called faith healer. She stated, "I have no healing power. I never healed anyone. I am absolutely dependent upon the power of the Holy Spirit." Like Oral Roberts, she worked closely with the medical profession. Kuhlman had a tremendous impact on Emily Gardiner Neal, a reporter who set out to debunk the healing ministry. Neal ended up herself with a full time ministry of healing in the Episcopal Church.

Then, there was Agnes Sanford, daughter of Presbyterian missionaries to China. She married an Episcopal priest, Edgar Sanford, in 1923. Her deep faith and theological vision left a lasting, positive impression on thousands.

The foremost Roman Catholic in the healing movement is Francis Macnutt who greatly influenced Dorothea Dudley, Methodist clergywoman, who in turn influenced our healing team here at Lindenwood Christian Church in 2004.

So here we are in our second year of worship services, Praise, Prayer, Holy Communion, and Healing. We are a part of the Christian Healing Ministry through the centuries.

I'm here because I was asked by a board member to work with the Healing Team to offer one more worship service for our congregation. So far, we have offered this service twenty-two times in 2005 and twelve times this year, 2006.

As I reflect on why I'm here it has to do with more than just being asked by Fred Boone. It has to do with my being healed from cancer in 1981. It has to do with a healing service here in the chapel several years ago when cancer of the thyroid gland was healed because of prayers and the laying on of hands. I'm here tonight because my friends shared with me and with those present on December 11, 2005 how God has brought healing to them.

One was healed from loneliness after the death of both parents. She was caused to meet a man who has made her life meaningful. Another friend was healed from chronic lung infection that almost claimed her life as a little girl. She was healed and later led to a young man who had been painfully shy with no social skills. God has used them to bless others many times in many ways. Another friend shared how God miraculously saved him and his son from a head on collision in East Tennessee. Another who lost both parents in 1937, who was cared for by Christian friends in a Christian Church in Kentucky, later survived serious lung surgery when she was 34 years old.

Still another dear friend who walked through a dark valley after losing a good job she had worked at for almost 20 years shared how God sustains her as she cares for a mother with Alzheimer's and a brother with cancer. Shadows in her life are seen as a sure sign that the light of Jesus is always shining.

I'm here because a dear, dear friend is healed from cancer of the Larynx. He had faith in God's power to see him through nine unbelievably difficult surgeries. Miraculously, a team of doctors rebuilt his esophagus and throat. The healing power of Christ Jesus touched him and continues to touch him. The faith of this dear one and his wife has inspired and continue to inspire all who know them. Miracles still happen. Unbelievable healings still occur.

A friend of mine shared with us how God healed his chronic back pain, the injuries suffered by his son, and the pains suffered by his wife.

I'm here because of a dear one who placed her hand on my incision in 1981 and trusted God. She also prays fervently for God's healing power, for family, and friends every day and night.

Isn't this why all of us are here? We believe! We know that God's healing power is available. Those who responded to a questionnaire in January of 2006 said, "Yes, I have experienced wholeness and healing in many ways at five-thirty pm on the 2nd and 4th Sundays. It's a special time for me."

The following are direct quotes:

- "What an authentic and simple approach to helping us become whole persons."
- "You can feel the presence of the Holy Spirit."
- "The messages are always uplifting, positive and appropriate to my life and my needs."
- "This service is different from all the others."
- "I was totally surprised by a sense of the presence of the Holy Spirit."
- "I felt really blessed by being able to share my prayer concerns verbally."
- "The warmth and the sense of being accepted was truly a blessing."

Some who have been constant in attendance have said:

- "I really feel better all over in every area of my life."
- "I seem to have a better mental attitude about giving and receiving forgiveness."
- "I have more peace of mind about making decisions."

Lindenwood's worship service of Praise, Prayer, Holy Communion, and Healing is a vital part of Christian Healing through the centuries.

Prayer

Loving God,

We thank you for your healing power in our lives. We thank you that we are privileged to share in this essential part of proclaiming the Gospel, the entire Gospel of our Lord Jesus Christ.

Amen.

Note

Most of the content of this chapter is from an excellent article on "Christian Healing in History" by Avery Brooke. It is found in the July/August 1991 issue of *Weavings: A Journal of the Christian Spiritual Life* pp. 6-19. Used by permission

Printed in the United States
151147LV00003B/18/A

9 780979 307973